WORLD WITHIN A SONG

WORLD
WITHIN
A SONG

Music That Changed My Life
and Life That Changed My Music

JEFF TWEEDY

DUTTON

DUTTON

An imprint of Penguin Random House LLC
penguinrandomhouse.com

DUTTON and the D colophon are registered trademarks
of Penguin Random House LLC.

Interior art © snorks/Shutterstock.com

LIBRARY OF CONGRESS CATALOGING-IN-PUBLICATION DATA
Names: Tweedy, Jeff, 1967– author.
Title: World within a song: music that changed my life and
life that changed my music / Jeff Tweedy.
Description: [1.] | New York: Dutton, 2023.
Identifiers: LCCN 2023028471 (print) | LCCN 2023028472 (ebook) |
ISBN 9780593472521 (hardcover) | ISBN 9780593472538 (ebook)
Subjects: LCSH: Tweedy, Jeff, 1967– | Popular music—Anecdotes. |
Alternative rock musicians—United States—Biography. |
Alternative country musicians—United States—Biography. |
LCGFT: Autobiographies.
Classification: LCC ML420.T954 A3 2023 (print) |
LCC ML420.T954 (ebook) | DDC 782.42166092 [B]—dc23/eng/20230804
LC record available at https://lccn.loc.gov/2023028471
LC ebook record available at https://lccn.loc.gov/2023028472
9780593475645 (signed edition)
9780593475652 (B&N signed edition)

Printed in the United States of America

1st Printing

BOOK DESIGN BY ASHLEY TUCKER

To Susie, Spencer, and Sammy

CONTENTS

LOOK . . .

I'M GOING TO LEVEL WITH YOU RIGHT OFF THE BAT. I don't know what I'm doing, and I probably don't have any business writing another book, much less one as conceptually conceived and philosophical as this one aims to be.

But the truth is, I should've written this book first, and I would have if I'd had any wherewithal and confidence from the get-go. So I wrote a memoir sort of by accident. Initially it was something proposed to me. Preposterous at first, considering I wasn't even half finished living my life by my own hopeful estimation. I was eventually convinced to give it a go, and I'm glad now that I was able to accept the task as a challenge as well as an opportunity to offer up a little advice in the form of "Here's some shit you might want to look out for if you're, like me, a human person trying not to suffer overly so" and "Hey, I'm a dumbass. Don't be a dumbass like me," along with a few "Well whaddaya know? I figured out some of this shit on my own, so you could try what worked for me so you don't have to go into the hospital and whatnot."

In the end I enjoyed it. I enjoyed it enough to write another book. This time I got a little closer to the stuff I think about the most and I allowed myself to revisit the topic I had the easiest time writing about in my memoir: the creative process. More specifically, I wrote about my own habit of intentionally making time for myself to spend a part of each day engaged with my imagination. I wrote about making stuff and how I think it's good and good for you.

I tried not to get too didactic or preachy in that book, but it was hard not to veer off into self-help-adjacent philosophy periodically. But honestly, I think it was the right thing to do. The way I see it, I'm lucky to be in a position to advocate for creativity as a live-well strategy. The world needs more of that type of thing, and I was happy to do it.

So that brings us to this book. The one you're holding or listening to right now. This book is the one I probably would have written first if I were more ambitious, and if I had been a little more clear-eyed about what I care most for in this world, and what I've thought about the most by far: other people's songs. And how much they have taught me about how to be human—how to think about myself and others. And how deeply personal and universally vast the experience of listening to almost anything with intent and openness can be. And most importantly, how songs absorb and enhance our own experiences and store our memories.

How did I come up with this particular list of songs? I could have easily chosen a thousand other songs to write about. And having finished that book, I would regret the omission of a thousand other songs. These are just the ones that came to me first. Besides, the specifics of the songs themselves aren't really the point. What's important to me to convey is how miraculous songs are. It doesn't matter how many people hear "A Day in the Life," there is only one version that belongs to you. Mine has little to do with yours. Our appraisals might align but I doubt your relationship to the song includes a memory of waiting for the doors to open at an all-ages Jodie Foster's Army concert on Laclede's Landing in St. Louis, with a flooding Mississippi River raging down Wharf Street and heaving up onto the steps of the Gateway Arch. Mind melting down on mushrooms, watching a husband-and-wife street-performing duo sing "A Day in the Life" while their toddler does laps around you keeping shockingly good time on a tambourine.

It'd be cool if we could see the worlds within the songs inside each other's heads. But I also love how impenetrable it all is. I love that what's mine can't be yours and we still get to call it ours. Songs are the essence of this condition. And in my opinion, they're the best way I know of to make peace with our lack of a shared consciousness.

Creating connection through music is my life's work. Truly. Still, what makes my thoughts on other people's songs worth investing in? Well, I'll tell you, if I hadn't written those other books, I'm not sure I'd be able to answer that. But what I've realized through sharing my thoughts and feelings in my books is that there are people out there having very similar thoughts and feelings. The lesson hasn't been that my perspective is so unique it must be shared so as to enlighten. It's more that I've learned that I'm not alone. I'm not a freak to care about this as much as I do.

The main response I get to the things I've written is the miraculous comment "I feel like I could have written that." It's a joyous discovery to realize that something as ego-driven and interior as a book can return from its visit to all the people it managed to reach in the world with the hopeful and humbling message that you've been understood. You've given someone else the words to name their own experiences. Wonders never cease.

A NOTE ON REMEMORIES

AS YOU PROGRESS THROUGH THIS BOOK, YOU'RE GO-
ing to encounter some dreamlike passages recounting
specific events in my life. I call them Rememories, and
I've been writing down some of my most-often-shared
life stories in that style for a few years now.

Their inclusion here has a couple of purposes. On
one hand, I hope that they'll work as palate cleansers
between chapters as we reemerge from the thick weeds
of my internal and endless musing on the weight of
songs, as we climb out of the "book-sized writing" language and look around for a little space to think.

But I also included them to illustrate how my deep
immersion in music has shaped how I really think and
remember things in "song-sized" thoughts and shapes.
And how important it is to allow the things we love the

most—the things we've contemplated the most thought-
fully and with the most empathy and compassion—to
guide our hand when we're stumped.

I have very few strongly held beliefs. Among them is
the conviction that loving one thing deeply and with
ardor is the best way to open yourself up to the world.
It's a bit counterintuitive, but I've seen it with my own
eyes and felt it with my own heart. My obsession with
music from a very early age had the potential to isolate
and alienate me from the world at large. But I believe
that by indulging that passion and focus, I found the
only way into knowing what people live for.

Loving one thing completely becomes a love for all
things, somehow. I've seen it in other people, too. And
I've been able to communicate with them solely using
the language I've learned from music to talk about, for
instance, other art, gardening, coaching college basket-
ball, war correspondence . . . you get the idea.

So I've included these memories, sung to the tunes
swirling around my own mind. They remind me of what
I'm getting at and how beautifully intertwined it all becomes over time when you open up and allow the world
to pour in both directions at once, inward and outward.

WORLD
WITHIN
A SONG

SMOKE ON THE WATER

I'D LOVE TO CLAIM THAT AT THE AGE OF SIX, HEAR-ing the brief passage of Mozart (incorrectly identified as Rachmaninoff) performed in the movie *Willy Wonka and the Chocolate Factory* was the catalyst that set me on my way to a lifetime of music-making . . . or that I was somehow introduced to some Jacques Brel or Leonard Cohen by an eccentric den mother at a Cub Scout meeting and I never looked back, having immediately absorbed the nuance and depth of the wordplay and how the simple melodic arcs embrace eternity . . .

In fact, I'd much prefer to have you believe just about anything other than what truthfully made the first dent in my musical mind. That's because the truth is that it was "Smoke on the Water" by Deep Purple. It kills me to admit this for a lot of reasons. Foremost of which is the fact that as I grew older and as this song maintained an ominous loitering presence on the airwaves of St.

Louis rock radio, it became more and more indefensible
as something I could admit to myself that I liked.

Things were different then. Without much else to
distinguish ourselves from each other as adolescents
(fewer clothing options, same shoes, our moms all cut
our hair), we were forced to broadcast our allegiances
(jock, nerd, sosh, etc.) by the music we professed to love.
By the time I was a full-blown teenager, this bong-
bruised, coughed-up lung of a song had evolved, in
terms of the people who liked it at the time, to signify a
distinct type of danger to a sensitive boy like myself.
Kind of the way some insects develop brightly colored
wings to tell predators, "Trust me, you're better off not
fucking with me." This song came to indicate a certain
toxicity, in other words.

But alas, I cannot deny its importance to me, and
countless others, as a budding musician. Because the
fact is, this riff (I'm not even sure I could speak to the
rest of the song considering how much I've avoided it in
the nearly fifty years since my first introduction; I know
it has something to do with Frank Zappa and some
semiautobiographical band exploit, but to me, even if I
HAD paid more attention to the words, this riff is so
dunderheaded and massive it blots out the sun—hippie
mumbo jumbo lyrics don't stand a chance) . . . this riff
is absolutely the first thing I ever played on a guitar, back
when I was seven or eight years old. This, my friends,
was the "Seven Nation Army" of my day. The likelihood

you could teach yourself these four notes on the bottom string of a guitar within a few minutes was very very high.

So I must bow to the rock gods. Who cares if it took a riff so demeaning and dumb to instill a little belief in myself as a potential musician? We all start somewhere. I started with "Smoke on the" goddamn "Water."

LONG TALL GLASSES

YOU KNOW, NOT EVERYTHING THAT ENDS UP HAVING a profound influence in your life is easily identified as enjoyable. In fact, I think I could safely argue that it's pretty rare for life lessons to be imparted free of concern and full of mirth. Songs, or at least most of the songs I've chosen to talk about here, are unique in that way. They really can teach with serenity, form wisdom while the mind drifts carelessly, or even shine a little light into the dark corners of a banging head.

But not always. There are still important kernels of knowledge that can only be whipped into us through discomforting experience. Take this Leo Sayer song, for example. Sure, it seems pleasant enough. And taken as a single dose, I'm almost certain one would recover fairly quickly from its mild toxins. But let's take this same song and play it . . . oh . . . let's say roughly forty-five times between six P.M. and nine P.M. on weekday evenings, and upward of seventy times a day on the weekends. Let's continue this ritual for several months and try to imagine the world-warping effect this little ditty might have on one's psyche.

If it weren't for the fact that I believe my father sincerely enjoyed such a routine, I would find it easy to subscribe to the possibility that the method behind such madness was in service to a DARPA program set up by the DOD to study the mind-altering potential inherent in repeated exposure to a single insipid storytelling pop song.

If you're unfamiliar with the song . . . first of all, CONGRATULATIONS . . . but I should give you a little outline of what its "deal" is. It's a musical tale of a man down on his luck (natch) who stumbles upon an establishment offering up food and drink to one and all. It goes on to describe said spread (which is where he unloads one of the most diabolically infuriating rhymes of all time: "There was ham and there was turkey / There was caviar / And long tall glasses / With wine up to . . . YAR"). It ambles along for a while before we get to the kicker: If he wants to partake in the bounty before him, he's gonna have to dance for it. But alas, he doesn't know how to dance, and he's sad, the music is sad, we're sad . . . but then . . . but THEN . . . Spoiler alert: Turns out he CAN dance after all.

Incredible. At this point in the song the refrain "You know I CAN'T dance," sung like a donkey doing a

Bogart impression, becomes "I CAN dance!" This is the moment where my beer maudlin-ed father would jump out of his chair and spill his Pabst (Extra Light) dancing and bellowing along. "I CAN DANCE!" EVERY. SINGLE. TIME.

So what did I learn from this hardship? Why am I writing about this particular song in a book designed to highlight the inspiration I've taken from the music I've consumed?

Well, I guess I'm not sure how to answer that. But I can tell you that at the time this was all happening, I was sure I was learning about things I would never do and ways that I would never be. As a musician, as a songwriter, as a father, and as a human, I guess.

Every now and then I throw this song on, and as I sit and listen, as this smug bauble of pop arcana winds its way through the paths in my mind that it's beaten down to dust, the memories of my father become so vivid I swear I can smell him. I am with him again. But this time without judgment. Only joy for his joy. Name something else in the world that can do that.

SPITTING ON THE
BAR MIRROR

REMEMBERING THAT OUR HOUSE, WHICH MY PARENTS claimed may have been a speakeasy at one time, had a bar in the basement, and a separate entrance, which checks out with its maybe being a place to drink during prohibition. It wasn't a totally finished basement, but it had an old, long bar, with a big mirror behind it, almost like an old saloon.

Bringing my friend downstairs and revealing my plan . . . I had seen a movie when I was a little kid where the bad guy spit at the bartender and spit on the mirror behind the bar. Based on this movie, my friend and I spent an entire afternoon running up to the bar, jumping on a bar stool, and spitting on the mirror behind the bar.

My father reacting in horror when he came home and saw the mirror, covered in our spit. I think that was the only time that he ever spanked me.

3

TAKIN' CARE
OF BUSINESS

IF YOU WERE A KID IN THE SEVENTIES AND HAD OLDER cousins who played guitar, there's a solid chance that your first exposure to a lot of songs was through an impromptu performance at a family barbecue or some other type of family get-together. And if you were like me, a little sheltered and radio-less, the idea that your cousins were incredible songwriters and musicians might have taken a strong hold.

For much of my childhood, I marveled at this song and how insanely good it was, and how incredible it was that my cousin (BeBo, we called him) wrote this masterpiece. This was my favorite of HIS songs. I'm not accusing him of plagiarism. I mean, it wasn't like he had a moral obligation to back-announce his selections on any given evening so that his weird little cousin wouldn't get the wrong idea about who wrote his material.

Thinking now about how many great songs he used

to play, I was tempted to write about Jim Croce and "Bad, Bad Leroy Brown" too, but then I remembered the night that particular illusion was destroyed by a newscast reporting on Croce's untimely death in a plane crash. As a montage of images from his career played over a medley of his hits, I put two and two together and figured out that Jim Croce was probably the one who wrote "Leroy Brown." But since they didn't play any Bachman-Turner Overdrive, I was able to retain my pride in being related to the guy who wrote "Takin' Care of Business."

It was a sweet time. I'm not particularly nostalgic for that era of my childhood, but I do appreciate that this way of hearing a song for the first time probably doesn't happen as much anymore. Maybe it does . . . I really don't know . . . but it seems like something that might have been extinguished by the relatively new relationship everyone has with music these days. It's omnipresent in all of our lives. Everyone is walking around with access to so much music it's hard to believe that when I finally did get a radio (one conveniently "fell off a train" at my dad's work somewhere around my ninth birthday), I used to stay up for hours hoping to hear a song a DJ might or might not ever play again, mostly because I didn't catch the name of the artist the first time around.

I truly hope that people still play songs for their extended younger kin without letting on who wrote what. Because a song's magic really does deserve to be spread around, and part ownership should definitely belong to whoever can conjure it up in front of any size audience spontaneously (okay, setting aside the chaotic publishing ramifications, of course).

The fact is, this song is probably one of the most important songs in my life. Because cousin BeBo took the time to learn it and sing it to his friends and family, and because it looked like a thing someone could do—write a song and sing it—I was convinced forever that writing a song and singing it was not only a way to tap into the divine, it was normal.

I'm not sure I've ever truly processed this song as anyone's other than my cousin's. And as I got older, a lot of people I knew would make fun of this band and this song. But there must be something to be said for the fact that every band I've ever been in knows this song. And how it's a not uncommon occurrence for someone to launch into this song for no particular reason at all during a sound check or rehearsal, to smiles all around when everyone joins in. In fact, there's a running gag at the Wilco headquarters and recording studio, the Loft. Whenever I try out a new guitar, the opening riff of "TCB" comes first. Mark Greenberg, our studio manager, drops whatever he's doing and runs to the nearest piano to play the pulsing high-register eighth notes that complete the ROCK!

It's pure joy every time. Any song that can put that much joy in the world deserves my respect.

Thank you, BeBo.

DON'T THINK TWICE, IT'S ALL RIGHT

BOB DYLAN. BOB. DYLAN. IS THERE ANYONE ELSE YOU can refer to with either of their names and be as sure someone will understand who you're talking about? I can't think of anyone. It's usually one or the other. Groucho Marx? I'll give you Groucho, but Marx is definitely a different dude. Anyway, what's left to say about Bob Dylan? Well, judging by the amount of shit written about him every year, a lot! Between the two big British rock mags, *Uncut* and *Mojo*, one or the other will put him on the cover at least once every six months. Presumably because people still can't get enough of the guy. Which makes sense, because I can't get enough of the guy, either.

In fact, I can't think of any other artist I love more. And whether they admit it or not (or in some cases whether or not they're even aware of it), I believe every songwriter wants some piece of what Dylan has. His poetic gifts, his prolificacy, his longevity, his mystique, his hair! He's like the guy who invented walking upright. Even if you don't know who he is, you should know you owe him a lot. I mean, I sure do. To Dylan, that is. And also the guy who invented walking upright.

So when it comes to all of the many attributes of Dylan's one could list or wish to possess, I would put myself down as a songwriter who longs for them all. Let's ignore the others who insist they are immune to the Dylan influence or that they exist freestanding apart from the world he has made for all of us song people. Because I, for one, think they are deluded poopie heads.

I could have easily chosen only Dylan songs to write about if I were only concentrating on the criterion of importance to my personal development as a writer of songs . . . but "Don't Think Twice" is the first Dylan song I fell for, so it's the one I'm including.

It was originally released on the album *The Free-wheelin' Bob Dylan*, in 1963. About four years before I was born. I first heard it on *Bob Dylan's Greatest Hits Vol. II*, which came out in '71. So I'm guessing I got this record in a cache of handed-down vinyl a few years after that. That puts us at around 1974. And that puts me at around seven years old. I mention all of this not to buff my bona fide badge as a precocious and intellectually curious youngster but because I still think about it, and I can still feel how deeply I identified with this song so quickly and how strange that is.

I once loved a woman
A child I am told
I gave her my heart but she wanted my soul

How does a seven-year-old hear that and say, "THAT'S ME!"? But I did. I did and I still do. How? My best guess now as to why a song kissing off a lover like this one would resonate with just about anyone is the fact that, at its core, it's saying, "I'll be okay. I'm alienated and maybe a bit angry that I could be treated so poorly, but guess what, I'm the one with the road in front of me. I am free."

How alienated could I have been as a seven-year-old to so desperately need to hear a Nixonian "You're not going to have me to kick around anymore" lyric as something more liberating than self-pitying? The answer is obviously VERY! I was born alienated, I think. And when I heard this song, it was maybe the first time I heard that hurt sung to a melody I could understand.

IS THERE A MERIT BADGE FOR SHAME?

EVERY TIME SOMEONE ASKS ME IF I WAS EVER A BOY Scout, I say no. And then I feel compelled to tell them I never made it on account of being shamed out of the Cub Scouts.

Here's the story.

I was pretty excited to build a Pinewood Derby car when they handed out the kits at our "den" meeting. It was supposed to be a father-son project, but (knowing how unlikely that scenario would be based on past experiences) I put it all together by myself when I got home.

Either my mom really got on my dad's case or my dad really did feel sorry for me when he saw my attempt at building a "race car." Or it's possible some combination of the above and his own competitive nature kicked in, because in a stunning reversal of attitude toward the whole idea, he committed to the undertaking with gusto.

Now, did that mean he took me down to an old workbench in the basement and carefully walked me through the steps of designing and shaping an aerodynamic miniature racing vehicle? No. If you were making a movie, I think this would be where you would cut together a montage of my father's coarse hands helping guide my chubby little fingers as they sand the contours of a Maserati out of a soft block of wood—paint being dabbed on my nose, heads tossed back laughing, sawdust falling to the floor, close-up on our eyes gliding along the sleek profile of a finished speedster.

But this is how it actually went. "BOY!! . . . BRING ME THAT DAMN 'CAR' YOU MADE DOWN HERE!! . . . NOW GO TO BED." Adding, "I get up before you know what day it is."

The next evening, Dad came home with a completely rebuilt masterpiece of engineering and design. Apparently, he had put a team of railroad technicians on the task. The axles were coated in graphite. They had hollowed out and filled an internal channel with mercury. And they had added a stack of tiny washers underneath the chassis so we could adjust the weight at the weigh-in, because they had determined being able to get as close as possible to the max weight would be the key to speed in a race being run with only gravity as fuel. To top it off, "my" car now sported a jaunty red, white, and blue paint job.

So far so good, right? Sure, some bonding with my

dad might have been nice, but this car really did "go like
the dickens," as my dad would say. "Our" car destroyed
the competition. Which, to be honest, mostly looked like
my car had before my dad Manhattan Project–ed the
shit out of that pathetic little chunk of crappy wood.

I admit it was really fun winning. And winning so
handily made it extra fun. Mercilessly, one might say. It
was a good night. And Dad was pretty excited to see the
trophy "he" won when we got home. No, he did not at-
tend. Need I remind you he got up "before the ass crack
of dawn"?

Okay. The real trouble started a year later.

Same drill. The bonding part of the project was em-
phasized as the most important part. A new block of
wood was issued with the clear directive that a new car
must be built to legally enter the contest.

I gave my dad the materials, this time without even
bothering to slap the wheels on the sucker, and I told
him to put the A team on it. "What's wrong with the
one from last year?" he asked. So I explained the rules to
him. He stared back at me and sucked on his teeth for a
few seconds, and then he said, "Well, gimme the old one
to take along so we can remember what we did to make
it so great."

Next evening he came home and handed me what
was obviously the same car as last year, only now it was
a glossy dark shade of blue. He winked. I nodded. He
was an adult. I was just a kid. We're geniuses, we thought.

The only person I told about our masterful plot to sidestep the rules and dominate the field for a second year running was my best friend at the time—let's just call him "Kent."

Well, as luck would have it, Kent came in second place. And as I stood holding my trophy, I watched Kent with tears in his eyes walk around the track, past the rows of lunch tables, and directly up to the lectern where our scout leader was making some final announcements for the evening over the PA. I can still vividly see him pointing in my direction as a small group of adults began to gather around him. Kent was a rat, turns out.

I mean, he was right. And I was wrong. I understood that even then. But it's what the adults did next that I still have trouble believing. The scout leader leaned into the microphone and made a terse request for me to step up to the lectern. Which is where my trophy was taken from my hands and I was officially disqualified. In front of everyone in attendance. All of my classmates.

I was inconsolable. My mother was irate. At them, thank god.

My dad was asleep when we got home. Understandable, considering he'd had "a whole got-damned day by the time you lift your pretty head off of your pillow."

He never said much about it other than, "Some people take stupid shit way too seriously."

I was never sure if he was talking about them or himself.

MULL OF KINTYRE

NOT A LOT OF PEOPLE ARE FAMILIAR WITH THIS SONG outside of the UK. Or at least that was the case in the late seventies. No way of telling these days. For all I know, some chunk of this tune is being used on TikTok, triggering a massive uptick in bagpipe sales to bored tweens. I doubt it. But weirder things have happened. It is gorgeous. Stirring, even. And I might have thought to include it here because it does exactly that—it stirs something Scottish in me. Something deep and ancestral. But if I'm being honest, a lot of Paul McCartney's music would have come to mind before this one if I were picking songs to write about based solely on my appreciation for them as a songwriter. But there's a story inside this song I'd like to share.

In spite of having been a massive hit on the UK charts as a single, it had never been on an album until late 1978, when it got its album debut on *Wings Greatest*.

Which I'm guessing was some type of contractually ob-ligated release, cobbled together for maximum Christ-mas sales. In other words, it never made its way onto a real album. But my story isn't that I found this cash grab of an album under the tree on Christmas morning and went on to fall in love with this oddly obscure track, which was a love letter to Sir Paul's home in the Scottish countryside. In fact, I had no knowledge this song or the *Wings Greatest* LP even existed until early summer 1979, when I received it as a gift from an unlikely source.

First, a little backstory.

There was a pivotal moment in my life I've written about before, which I'd like to recount here a bit as well—the catastrophic bicycle accident I had on the last day of school before summer break in 1979. In my memoir and elsewhere, I've often credited this terrible childhood event and the forced isolation that resulted from it (due to injuries sustained) as the main reason I learned how to play guitar. A skill that forever changed the trajectory of my life. This is a tangential story to that main narrative—a soft, sweet memory, but indelible nonetheless.

The friend I was with when this accident happened was a very different kind of kid than I was. He was more of a country kid. We didn't have a lot in common other than baseball, maybe. He was kind of an acquaintance, really, but we liked each other enough to "go bike riding" after school that day. So it wouldn't have been surprising to me at all if I had never seen him again after the trauma he went through, seeing me carted off to the hospital in the back of his neighbor's pickup truck with a blood-soaked towel wrapped around the gaping holes in my thigh. We'd been racing our bikes up and down a hill in front of his house. I had his little brother riding double behind me on a banana seat, clutching my ribs, when I crashed into a drainage ditch. His little brother walked away without a hair out of place. I got skewered by some rusty metal retaining rods sticking out of an old culvert. My friend rode up laughing at the spectacle of us sailing off of the end of his blacktopped cul-de-sac into oblivion. And then quickly went white when he saw my horrific wounds. That was the last time I saw him.

Until about three weeks later, when he showed up at my house to keep me company while I was stuck in bed. He had brought me a get-well-soon present. *Wings Greatest.* I had no idea he knew music was my "thing," and I remember being so touched by how attentive my friend was. Music definitely wasn't his thing. I'm not sure what his thing was, but judging by his preferred after-school activities and his affinity for vehicular speed, I'm assuming adrenaline was his thing.

But I remember feeling truly uplifted and "seen," as we say today. It just felt so completely perfect and not accidental. It wasn't a wild guess. He had thought about it. And his thoughtfulness had led him to a truly personal gift for his laid-up friend. I mean, compared to the jigsaw puzzles and stuffed animals ("For the thousandth time, I'm allergic to dust, people!") from my relatives, you'd think this kid was the closest friend I ever had. But he wasn't. He was just a sweetheart who cared about people enough to listen to them when they talked about things he wasn't as interested in. You know, a good person.

We never really crossed paths again. I think he moved and ended up at a different school. But I think about him every time I hear "Mull of Kintyre" and how great it felt to have someone see me the way I was just beginning to see myself. Especially at a moment in my life where my true identity felt so hidden and invisible to others. And I'm also always reminded to keep working on my ability to pay attention to people in a way that would lead me to their *Wings Greatest* if they ever needed some warmhearted cheering up. It's a good way to be.

LOUD, LOUD, LOUD

IF YOU'VE EVER WONDERED WHAT A MANSON FAMILY–led community theater troupe would sound like rehearsing a copyright-avoiding knockoff mash-up of *Hair* and *Jesus Christ Superstar* (let's call it *Jesus Hair*), I think I have some good news for you.

Aphrodite's Child's *666* is your ticket. I think it's just about the wildest, most over-the-top, one-of-a-kind, and insane rock concept album ever made. The audacious conceits and pretensions of the Who's *Tommy* sound perfectly reasonable by comparison. "They should've called it *Timmy*," I said to myself once, deep in the throes of *666* reverie.

The album was recorded in late 1970 and early 1971 by Vangelis and a crazy cast of Greek luminaries (including Irene Papas) that apparently disbanded before the album was finally released in 1972. The lyrics are supposedly based on the Book of Revelation. And I'm

WORLD WITHIN A SONG

sorry, but that's the best I've ever been able to muster by way of offering up a coherent synopsis. I can tell you it's one of my favorite albums of all time and my physical copy is one of my most prized possessions.

So how did I end up with this tortured slab of surreal (Dalí was a fan!) European counterculture prog? Well . . . have you ever heard of cargo cults? Those remote uncontacted groups living on islands in the Pacific that would form societies and religions around the mysterious items that would wash up on their beaches? Most often these items had been provided by "sky gods" (i.e., planes)— miscalculated supply drops and downed aircraft and equipment from as early as World War II. Yes, it's a stretch, but I totally relate to how something like that could work. Because although I grew up solidly middle-class in an American small town with access to the world through televisions and phones and a relatively modern existence, I have to say I know what it feels like to have something incomprehensible practically land on my head: a full crate of my older brother's mysterious and eclectic record collection. Gifted to me in exchange for a promise to never order records from the Columbia House record club.

In 1976, these felt like the kinds of records no other nine-year-old in the world would have been (or should have been) listening to. LPs by Amon Düül II, Kraftwerk, and Tangerine Dream, to name just a few. And, of course, 666, the subject of this piece. Now, almost fifty years later, it's still a pretty adventurous cross-section of

recorded history. And I didn't just own them, I LIS-
TENED to them. I learned them. I formed an internal
culture warped by the cosmic experiment of giving an
anomalous set of references to an unworldly though
curious musical mind. (I always think that these records,
combined with my aunt's and my older sister's [also in-
herited] Monkees and Motown seven-inch records, succinctly explain almost every musical move I've ever made.)

As a way to honor this bountiful box—this seeming
Rosetta stone to a language I had no idea had never been
spoken—I could have picked a number of songs off this
album as representative. Like "The System," with its simultaneously naughty and invigorating (to a nine-year-
old) chorus, "We got the system to FUCK the system!"

But this is the song I've returned to the most.

"Loud, Loud, Loud."

Let me set the scene. In your mind's eye (ear?), picture these lyrics spoken by the most painfully earnest
young woman's voice you can imagine (I used to always
picture Manson-ite Patricia Krenwinkel reciting these
words before I learned through researching this book
that it's actually Daniel Koplowitz, the young son of a
diplomat) over what sounds like someone learning how
to alternate between two simple chords on a piano.

The day the walls of the cities will crumble away
Uncovering our naked souls

We'll all start singing . . .
Shouting . . .
Screaming . . .

A chorus of unmistakably dissociated voices joins in with a four-note descending chant.

Loud, loud, loud, loud

You can almost hear the matching tracksuits.

The day the circus horses will stop turning around
Running fast through the green valleys
We'll sing . . .
And cry . . .
And shout . . .
Loud, loud, loud, loud

We're marching into the flames now, people. Eyes fixed on the smoldering horizon . . .

The day the cars will lay in heaps
Their wheels turning in vain
We'll run along the empty highways
Shouting . . .
Screaming . . .
Singing . . .

Chorus getting . . . um . . . louder now . . .

Loud, loud, loud, loud
The day young boys will stop becoming soldiers
And soldiers will stop playing war games
We'll sing and cry and shout

Tension building . . .

Loud, LOUD, LOUD, LOUD
The day will come up
That we'll all wake up

Yes! That's how powerful this song is. Not every song can take a hit like rhyming *up* with *up*.

Hearing the shout of joy
And shouting together with the freaks

This word "freaks." I had no business identifying with this word as a nine-year-old. And I probably shouldn't claim it now. But the heart knows what the heart knows.
And it continues . . .

The day the world will turn upside down
We'll run together 'round and 'round
Screaming . . .

Shouting . . .
Singing . . .

Still escalating . . .

Loud, loud, loud, loud
Loud, loud, loud, loud
Loud, loud, loud, loud

Is this song silly? Undeniably. Do I still get goose bumps? Every single time. And I think that's the point worth making here. I don't think you should ever override what your body is telling you about a song. Life's too short to let your critical thinking get in the way of being moved by music. I mean, what's more important? Catharsis? Or feeling intellectually superior to someone else's art?

By the way, on the album this song cross-fades into Demis Roussos's unmistakable hornlike voice singing the opening lyrics of "The Four Horsemen." And if you're listening to these tracks along with the book, I highly recommend continuing through this song as well and treating yourself to possibly (at the proper volume) the most exciting drum fills ever recorded.

Fuck yeah!

OLIVER GOTHIC

WHEN I WAS AROUND NINE YEARS OLD MY MOTHER read about something called "Tree House Camp" in the local paper, noticed that it was very close to where she worked, and enrolled me for the upcoming summer "session."

The picture in the ad looked like it might have been a still from *Swiss Family Robinson*. The elaborate wooden chalets and walkways between them, all suspended in some type of forest canopy that looked like none of the wooded areas I'd ever seen in my neck of the . . . um, wooded areas . . . did raise some suspicion. Something about it reminded me of the disgusting jar of briny water that sat on my bookshelf, the one that was clearly never going to transform into an adorable family of "Sea-Monkeys."

But like any kid my age, the dream of inhabiting a space among the squirrels and birds, separate from, and above, the ground-dwelling adults—it was all intoxicating and drowned out any alarm bells that my (and I'm assuming my mother's) better judgment should have set off.

We arrived the morning of the first day at a fallow field on the outskirts of town—overgrown but decidedly flat and treeless. My mother, who I'm sure was late for work and had very much intended to drop me off with little more than what you would call a rolling stop, decided she needed to park the car, get out, and ask someone the question that was on both of our minds:

"Where are the fucking trees!?"

"See over there? Them trees popping up just beyond the horizon? That's where the camp is. We own all this land but this here spot is the closest we can get a car for dropping off the kids."

"Ah, okay," my mother said, nodding, "makes sense."

"Does it?" I thought as we began the long walk through the weeds and I watched my mother's car disappear over my shoulder. As she waited for a break in the traffic to pull out, I was quickly calculating if the distance I'd walked so far was already past the point of no return, alongside how furious she'd be if I bailed. Too late. As she made it out onto the road, she looked back, saw me looking at her, and gave a chipper little toot on her horn that I found unconvincing. I knew I was doomed.

"First thing we gotta do is clear this brush . . . ," said

the dour, sun-dried, semi-toothed, drifter-type gentle-
man handing me a machete, "so we can get up to them
trees and start to buildin'."

By mid-June, when this was all happening, the
heat and humidity in southern Illinois is brutal, even in
the morning. Inhospitable. Even to a dumb kid who
was decades away from being softened by central air-
conditioning. Which, by the way, was a topic I often
heard my folks discussing as something they would be
able to afford once I got a job and left the house or went
away to college. Again, I was nine.

So I definitely remember being way too hot. But the
rest of my memory of this episode is muddy. And, although it has the distinct weight and knurled texture I
associate with trauma, I have almost zero direct images
attached to this short chapter in my life beyond the ini-
tial drop-off and my preteen mental confirmation of a
swindle.

Basically, the con was to get a bunch of kids to clear
some land. Kind of ingenious, really. Diabolical even.
And when you consider the fact that they had charged
our parents for our services as opposed to . . . oh, I don't
know . . . PAYING ANYTHING AT ALL, you begin
to clearly see some real Mark Twain–type scoundrels. I
mean, if you weren't around in the midseventies, let me
tell you, kids my age would mow a football-field-sized
lawn with a push mower for a couple of bucks. Happily!

So, again, the people who concocted this whole scheme were some grade-A sociopaths.

Oddly, I also don't remember much about the other kids. I don't think there were many of us. I have a vague memory of us all mirthlessly holding our implements: hoes, rakes, shovels, hatchets, saws, machetes, and scythes, like the cast of *Oliver!* crossed with *American Gothic*.

What I do remember is that this was the last time my mother ever made an effort to push me out of the nest. I know she felt bad when she picked me up, sunburned and angry, later that afternoon.

So I ended up going to work with my mother a lot that summer. She worked at a cabinet place and I'd spend the day pretending I lived in the display kitchens and bathrooms. Sometimes I'd climb around on the massive rolls of carpeting in the warehouse. But that activity usually ended with my eyes burning and itching, watering, turning red, and sometimes even swelling shut. Mom said it was the chemicals they sprayed on the carpeting to make it "safe." She thought I might be allergic to them, because it didn't bother her. But I also didn't see her rolling around on them.

When we would leave to go home that summer, my mom would often swing by the site of the "Tree House Camp" just to see what kind of fun I might be missing and if there were any actual tree houses being built.

We never saw any.

BOTH SIDES NOW

THERE ARE SOME SONGS SO PERFECT IT'S IMPOSSIBLE to imagine them ever not existing. Melodies so seamless that it makes no sense to contemplate how they were constructed. Miniature suns and moons. Here long before us, and sure to survive long after we're gone. Music that arrives not as something new but as something that finally has a name. This song feels like it's been a part of me for as long as I've had a me to feel.

It seems certain that I must have heard this song as an infant. Judy Collins's version was riding high on the charts shortly after my first birthday, so it's not unlikely that it would have seeped into my consciousness around the same exact time my developing mind's language centers were just kicking into gear. If that's the explanation for this feeling I have that this song is purely a geological fact, then lucky me. What a gift it's been to have this song on speed dial my entire life. I can't always remember all the words, but the melody is always there. It almost feels like it has a specific physical presence. With its own unique feeling. Like a grade school locker-lined hallway. Or maybe it's more like a loved one's face. Like how I can close my eyes and see my sister as a young woman getting married, then later, smiling beneath silver-gray bangs. Like how both those images ARE my sister to me, wherever I am in the world.

It's love that I'm describing, isn't it? I trust this song so much. Its wisdom, lyrically, is astonishing. And as simple as it may sound, "Something's lost, but something's gained / In living every day," when combined with such an indelible melody, is a pretty remarkable bit of consolation to have coming out of your radio. And, in turn, on a loop in your head for more than fifty years. How? Joni Mitchell was barely out of her teens when she wrote this song. So again I ask, how? Pure magic. Pure genius.

If somehow you aren't familiar with this song, please go listen to it now if you can. Trust me, you need it. And if it doesn't keep you company for a long time, I hope you have a song that feels, to you, the way I've described this one. I'd be lost without it.

So . . . It's a good thing it can't be taken away from me. Not even if I never heard it again. It is a part of the world I live in. Like air and water.

8

LUCKY NUMBER

GROWING UP BEING MY MOM'S BEST FRIEND HAD
some perks. She was a night owl. Liked watching old
movies and didn't particularly care if I ever went to bed
as long as I got up in the morning to go to school. With
hindsight it's now clear that some boundary-setting and
better sleep hygiene would have saved me a fortune in
counseling. But if that had been the case, who knows
where I'd be. Happier? Who's to say. I do know that I
probably would have never been exposed to some great
Judy Garland and Mickey Rooney movies without that
loose structure.

And if had kept normal kid hours in 1979, there's a
good chance I would have missed one of the most important television events of my lifetime: the all–"New
Wave" episode of *The Midnight Special*. First of all, where
I grew up in southern Illinois we watched St. Louis TV
stations, and the "Midnight" part of *The Midnight*

Special meant two A.M. on either Friday or Saturday night. That's how low in the programming hierarchy this syndicated music program was. They didn't even feel like they had to honor the time advertised right there in the title.

Mom usually controlled the clicker (actually I'm pretty sure we didn't have a TV remote yet—point is, we watched what she wanted to watch as a rule), but she was pretty good about letting me watch music programs because she knew how much they meant to me. To be honest, these shows were usually kind of a drag; I hated about 75 percent of the acts they'd have on. Pablo Cruise on *Don Kirshner's Rock Concert*? No thank you! I'm twelve. Cocaine, I know not what it is. But something is making you all look like my grandmother's standard poodle in need of a walk.

Not on this night, though. Check out this lineup— the Cars! (live), Suicide! (doing "Dream Baby Dream" and "Ghost Rider" LIVE!), the Records (meh), and Iggy Pop ("Five Foot One" and "I'm Bored"!), along with clips by M ("Pop Muzik," a 45 rpm I bought with my own money) and Lene Lovich doing "Say When" and "Lucky Number."

That's a big night for a kid looking for anything that can match the weirdness and excitement of the odd "cargo cult" crate of records stashed away in his bedroom. I wanted mind-warping stuff. It's what I had unreasonably come to expect for my entertainment dollar. I could probably make an equally compelling case for almost any of the songs I heard that night for the first time (minus the Records' set).

They all made indelible impressions, but I think Lene Lovich's song "Lucky Number" still feels like the most poignant reminder of that late night to me. More so because of my mother's reaction than my own. She lit up at Lene's eccentricity. Something about the combination of her old-world costume and bizarre modern mannerisms got my drowsy mother to sit up and pay attention in a way none of the male-dominated acts had achieved.

"She's different," was her assessment on the whole. "Lucky Number" was the bigger hit in my mother's estimation of Lovich's two songs. She liked it so much that she helped me find the record at Venture that weekend. Miraculously, we found a copy of Lovich's debut album, *Stateless*. To be honest, this reaction and strong endorsement of such a weird performer puzzled me a bit at the time. I loved the song because it was exciting and bold music with odd angular melodic jumps that felt almost like another song from some other dimension was periodically interrupting, like an impatient kid in the lunch line at school, jumping ahead to grab the last slice of pizza.

In hindsight, the reasons for my mother's apparent affinity for this particular tune have become much more obvious to me. My mother often offered up this bit of tragic advice to me: "You're born alone and you'll die alone, so you might as well get used to being alone." She was a brilliant woman, but this is obviously a grim outlook on life that someone with a bit more awareness of healthy boundaries would have kept a million miles away from a sensitive young lad like myself. It made me sad then. And it still makes me sad, knowing how born of experience that aphorism must have been for my mom. And in some way, I'm sure, protecting herself with this shield of bullshit must have helped keep her sane.

But on this night more than forty years ago, I watched her hear someone else sing "My lucky number is ONE." I saw it with my own eyes. She lit up at the idea that someone else, even someone as weird as Lene Lovich, could understand where she was coming from. My mom heard herself. I'm sure of it now. And it makes me happy to know that whether she made the connection or not, in that moment she was not alone. She never was.

HAT-WEARING KIND OF GUY

NOTICING THAT MY LOUD, DRUNK FRIEND HAD GONE uncharacteristically silent while cutting my hair, after I'd been talked into a rattail at his insistence. My eyes focusing on a bedroom dresser mirror one room across from the kitchen table where I sat, as it slowly dawned on me that his mute status was due to a violent laughing fit that had bent him over against the wall, gasping for air, as he surveyed his handiwork. He had unilaterally decided my hair wasn't quite long enough for a satisfying rattail, so he had elected to shave upward toward the tops of my ears on either side of my scalp. Giving me what looked like the haircut equivalent of a coonskin cap. Summer school began the following day.

. . . I've always been a hat-wearing kind of guy.

GLORIA

"JESUS DIED FOR SOMEBODY'S SINS BUT NOT MINE."

Has there ever been a more attention-grabbing first line of a record? Patti Smith's album *Horses* was yet another providence-delivered document slipped under the door of the mental cage that was late-seventies small-town life, via my brother's gifted stash.

Hearing these words in the environment I lived in, at the age I heard them, felt dangerous. Without exaggeration. I was born a skeptic. And my suspicion of organized religion grew as I grew. It's hard to describe the innate revulsion the idea of going to church instilled in me. Witnessing a couple of my cousins transform from being totally fun to be around to absolutely terrifying monomaniacal Jesus freaks didn't help with the paranoia.

Religion was something I feared catching like a flu. Or being bit by a vampire bat. I had no idea how to

protect myself from what appeared to be such an ir-
rational mindset befalling me. How did it happen? Was
marijuana (which I had a vague awareness of, courtesy of
these same slightly older relatives) truly a gateway drug?
I had no idea how to remain vigilant, except to reaffirm
to myself on a regular basis that things did not add up. I
remember thinking to myself, "If Jesus is so great, why
are you (a person who I used to really like) such a pain
in the ass to be around?"

Luckily, my mom and dad were decidedly lax about
churchgoing. Easter? You bet. Christmas? Midnight
mass seems like a long shot. Let's play it by ear and keep
tabs on Dad's beer intake. And that was about it. That is,
until I reached confirmation age. For some reason they
insisted I start going to Sunday school and studying to
be confirmed. With the welcome caveat that if I finished
my confirmation and took communion, I could then
choose whether or not I ever stepped foot in church
again.

St. Paul United Church of Christ was the congrega-
tion they had both attended since they were kids. It was
the chapel where I had been christened. So in theory, I
understood the request. In practice, it was painful.

Before I get too far ahead of myself, let me say I'm as
confused as you are about the denomination. People
would always ask me what denomination I was growing
up. And I'd say, "Christian." And they'd go, "Duh!
What kind of Christian?" And I'd say, "Ummm . . . the

United Church of kind?" To which they might reply, "But I thought you were going to take communion. Aren't you Catholic then?" And I'd say, "Ever since my sister had holy water thrown on her at a sleepover and came home scared she was going to hell, my mom has been pretty negative about Catholics, so I don't think that's it."

The truth is, my mom came by her own religious skepticism the good old-fashioned way. Growing up, her bedroom window was situated directly behind a convent and a seminary. She always claimed the traffic between the two—the trysts and the general sneaking around—kept her awake at night. "They're all a bunch of phonies," she'd say. But I only heard these stories later. At the time we're talking about, she was biting her tongue, determined not to put her finger on the scale of my salvation, I guess. Of course, my true salvation was one no one could save me from. Mostly because they had no better chance of understanding my deliverance from the dark than I had of understanding theirs. I've often heard Patti Smith described as a punk priestess. Which leads me to believe that I'm not alone in marking my first introduction to her voice as a rapturous event. A conversion of sorts. I already had a passion for music. But until I heard this song (and the thirty-five minutes or so of rock that followed), I'm not sure I understood catharsis or the terrifyingly transformative power an individual performer can possess. Every line of lyric a shard of poetry sung with the spirit and cadence of a taunt. Whatcha gonna do about it?!

> *Thick heart of stone*
> *My sins my own*
> *They belong to me, ME*

God, how I dreamed about one day standing up for myself, unafraid of not fitting in. I still dream of possessing Patti's fearlessness, but that's beside the point. I needed this music. I'm lucky it found me at such an early age. Any later might have been too late. Some might describe this event as divine intervention. It's a concept that is hard to argue with.

AS IF IT ALWAYS HAPPENS

SLOVENLY WAS A BAND ON SST RECORDS. SST, IF YOU don't know, was an independent punk rock record label. In fact, it was probably the first non-major label any of us kids walking around calling ourselves "punks" in the early eighties had ever really heard of. In the truest spirit of DIY, Black Flag founding guitarist Greg Ginn repurposed the company he had started when he was twelve to sell homemade ham-radio electronics (SST stands for Solid State Tuners) into a record label so the band could put out their own music. And they quickly realized that a lot of their less enterprising and not as "together" friends could use some help getting their records out, too.

And as it turned out, pretty much all of their friends had something incredible to share with the world, musically. For a while, it felt like every record I bought was on SST, and everything I listened to influenced my own music. Minutemen! All-timers. Meat Puppets! Where would I be without them? Hüsker Dü! Um, have you ever heard Uncle Tupelo? On and on it continued . . . Sonic Youth, Dinosaur Jr., all extremely important records. Not just to me. Whether you're aware of it or not, these are the records that shaped a lot of your favorite bands.

Sounds like hyperbole. It's not. Tell me some of your favorite records and I feel confident I could draw a direct connection to at least one SST release. The label had a batting average so high my friends and I started doing something we'd never even considered before—buying records by bands we'd never heard of based only on SST's ostensibly liking them enough to put their record out. We had all rolled the dice based on a cool album cover, sure . . . and it wasn't unheard of to hand over some cash based on a terrific band name (Butthole Surfers comes to mind). It seemed absurd to buy a record only because it was on a label like Columbia or Warner Bros., but SST felt so deeply curated and reliable that we all ended up being the kind of record consumer who would scour the bins flipping records over, looking for their logo.

I keep saying "we" because I want it to be known that as I've gotten older and traveled around, and met more and more musicians, I've come to understand that what initially felt like a unique personality trait was in reality something I had in common with way more people than I would have ever been able to understand in those pre-internet days. I was perfectly normal back in my early teens, albeit a little lonely and obsessed. Would have been nice to know that back then, but an equally likely guess is that it might have destroyed me to feel a little less special.

One of the ways I could have figured out how much I had in common with others might have been by understanding the principles of marketing, even just a little bit. Because when SST began negating the need to hunt for their imprint by affixing stickers emblazoned with their logo to their shrink-wrapped front covers, the writing really was on the wall. My reaction at the time was devoid of suspicion. It saved me time. I kept buying pretty much anything they put out.

And then, the laws of free-market capitalism began to be applied. It seemed like the more SST records I bought, the more they would release. Eventually it was financially impossible to keep up. So I was forced to regain a more scrutinizing style of buying records. Not before I found myself owning decidedly less classic albums, by the likes of Lawndale and Zoogz Rift. Fun records to own. I still have them. But let's just say they're nonessential.

So where am I going with all of this indie label lore? Slovenly. That's where I'm heading. SST put out their album *Riposte (a Little Resolve)* right in the middle of my SST spending spree. And to a lot of people, most of my friends included, this record landed somewhere on the downward slope of our ability to trust quality to the logo alone. Not me, though. I have listened to this record as much as almost any other record I own. I get that the singing, especially, wasn't an easy sell for a lot of people. Ian Curtis by way of California isn't far off.

But for me, this record sums up my feelings and affinity for do-it-yourself beauty. In essence, this song is an ecstatic poem about an epiphanous moment in the park—"Being with all of those . . . BAAAY-BIES"— read over some uniquely latticed post-punk guitars. It weaves and swoons. Stops abruptly like a hand slapping a desk and resumes with a sigh.

This is aspirational art. Aimed squarely at catharsis. There is no reason for this music to exist outside of those very lofty goals. This music aims at a purpose high above commerce, popularity . . . I can hardly bring myself to say stardom. It's unabashed in its artistic ambition. It's a few people of similar ages and mindsets—friends— allowing themselves to be vulnerable as a collective. Without much promised in the way of reward, other than to have some music to listen to that no one else could make but them. The ultimate dream for me, ever since this record taught me to dream in this way. With my friends. In whichever direction we choose.

TERRY

THE ONLY BONA FIDE FIRST-WAVE PUNK ROCKER IN my hometown of Belleville, Illinois—a man we'll just refer to as Terry—insisting to a teen me that "noise music" is the only thing worth listening to. Teen me mail-ordering Psyclones' *Cult Leader Gang-Raped by Disciples* cassette-only release—featuring a man having his mouth forcibly opened and pissed in on the hand-folded cardboard insert cover. Dropping news of my recent purchase into some casual record store counter conversation mere weeks later, where Terry vehemently denounces "noise music"—"Noise music is fraud, man. POP music is all I listen to. But not like the Beatles! The Monkees, MAN! The Beatles are pretentious bullshit. Monkees are pure pop! Noise is over. You gotta get into POP!"

Teen me realizing Terry is a dangerous person.

SOMEWHERE OVER
THE RAINBOW

WHEN I WAS GROWING UP, AROUND SEVEN OR EIGHT years old, I thought I knew the Cowardly Lion. Better yet, I thought my sister was going to get engaged to him, and I remember being giddy at the thought of having such an esteemed family member.

I admired my sister for being able to land such a big fish. But it turned out he was just a local actor who had played the part a few times in a local repertory theater and liked doing his best Bert Lahr impression for impressionable little kids. The dream really fell apart when I was dragged to see him perform as Willy Loman in *Death of a Salesman* at a St. Louis dinner theater, IN THE ROUND. Not long after, he and my sister broke it off. He went on to star in a pretty major ad campaign for Burger King as a character they had created named Herb. Researching it, it appears that there were several Herbs, separated by regional markets. The bit was based on the slogan "Where's Herb?" He'd be in local commercials as Herb and then they'd send him out to cause a stir by showing up at Burger Kings around the Midwest. It was a simpler time. Still, he and my sister remained on good terms, so we were all proud of him.

It's a strange memory to associate with something so sublime, but that's the truth of where my mind goes when I hear "Somewhere over the Rainbow." I always think of "Herb," or "what's his name," as my dad called him.

And then I think of my mother. Sitting up on the couch with me very late in the night, watching Judy Garland movies in our pajamas. My mother watching Judy sing. Me watching my mom, through the TV-lit blue twists and curls of her cigarette smoke, become as soft as a child, mouthing along silently, eyes wide, fully transported. Loving her so much and being so happy to see her look so different, knowing even at that age how important it was for her to get to be somewhere else, if only for a moment.

It's as perfect a memory as I have of my mother, and it's a perfect song. No one will ever write one better.

DEATH OR GLORY

THERE WAS A BRIEF PERIOD IN THE EARLY EIGHTIES when the older of my two brothers lived in a small but nice apartment on the Upper West Side of Manhattan with his wife at the time. I won't go into the details of how that came to be. Because I don't really remember them. But it had something to do with his wife being on an executive fast track with some big-time accounting firm. My first-ever introduction to New York City was when my mom and I went to visit them. We got the typical tourist impressions at the time. Central Park is wonderful. Subways are loud. And holy shit, I've never seen so many people in my life.

But the thing about that trip that left the deepest, most indelible mark on me was seeing street musicians for the first time. Violinists, steel drummers, classical guitarists, pianists, everywhere. In the park, in the subway, ON the subway cars. To me, a super-curious, budding romantic artist type, it was exhilarating witnessing people laying out their hats and guitar cases to collect coins and the occasional paper money. "I see"— jotting down a mental note—"they appear to be paying their dues."

But the intimidating part, the part I've thought about a lot since that first encounter with the largeness of everything, is that those same musicians also indirectly informed me of my own smallness. They were all so good. Invariably, my mom and I would walk away shaking our heads in disbelief at the musicianship we'd just witnessed. Just astonished at there being so much talent, and then thinking if this is just what the street has to offer, what on earth are they doing in places like Carnegie Hall? It was uplifting, because it's always uplifting to be in the presence of an artist being great at what they do. But boy, did it hammer home how bad I sucked at the guitar.

Another takeaway—a realization that must have been subliminally received at my mother's side in the eighties, a bit of wisdom about how the world operates that has slowly been working its way toward the front of my brain for decades now until this very moment—is how invulnerable all the musicians were. They dressed how they pleased and poured their hearts out in the public square. Where I grew up, both of those traits could get you a solid beating, or at the very least a healthy dose of merciless ridicule. It wouldn't have mattered how good you were at your flute, jackass. How were they unafraid and safe from that ugliness? I wanted to feel like that. Where does one sign up for that kind of moxie, I wondered. The answer is the city. The city has the power to inoculate one against judgment. The bigger the better. Everyone's busy. Everyone has seen it all. The more people there are, the less power any one group has to shame people into the shadows.

So what did this subtle transmission communicate to this wide-eyed sponge on a cellular level? I asked my mom if she would buy me a beret. And she did. She even told me repeatedly how much she loved it when I wore it the rest of the trip. I felt bold in it. More myself. Or at least, wearing a beret made me feel like a person I had a hand in inventing.

It felt good. It didn't last. I have a vivid memory from when I got back home of having my beret on, hopping out of my mom's car after getting dropped off at school, then realizing within seconds the catastrophic miscalculation I was making, blithely ambling into a buzz saw of humiliation. Then, in one swift motion, wiping that ridiculous round puff of felt off the top of my head and into my bag. It didn't happen if no one saw it. Death or glory indeed!

So what does this have to do with "Death or Glory" the song—how do the Clash figure into this biographical miniature? Well, aside from the fact that the only reason I could have possibly wanted a beret was because

I saw the Clash wearing them, I think this story is kind of at the very core of who I am. It illustrates the still-constant battle I have between the learned suspicion of my own desire to feel liberated and my deep natural need to actively create, not just works of art but who I am, through discovery by way of trial and error.

If you've ever seen me perform, I'm sure it's obvious that every time I walk up to the edge of showmanship I say something stupid like, "As far as audiences go, you guys are okay. And that's saying something because I don't really like audiences. In fact, statistically there are only about three or four of you I'd want to hang out with." That's the internal seesawing at work. That's Belleville Jeff jumping in and interrupting Beret Jeff. "Imma let you finish, but berets make you look like a pretentious acorn."

The Clash symbolizes all of this to me more than any other band I've loved. They make me cringe. I cringe at wanting to be them. But I still love them. Like family. They made me who I am, but that's not all as lovely as it might imply.

SCHADENFREUDE
BUFFET

WHEN I WAS GROWING UP, EACH MEMBER OF MY
family absolutely detested their counterpart in our next-
door neighbors' family. The Winkers. My mom avoided
the mom. Dad thought the dad was a phony. My
brothers had a beef with the son. And the daughter was
my nemesis. No idea what happened to make it so. It
just was, and everyone accepted that we hated each other.

Every once in a while there would be some thawing
of relations. A detente. Christmastime seemed to put
everyone on their best behavior, for example. Never
lasted long. One day, shortly after Christmas 1978, Rufus, the oldest son, whom my parents only ever referred
to as "Dufus" (us being a unified front when it came to
talking shit about the Winkers), was pacing around in
their backyard talking into some kind of walkie-talkie,
looking up at the sky. My dad pulls up in the driveway
that divided our two backyards. Home from work, gets

out of his "company" car. Sees Rufus acting weird and shouts over at him, "Whatcha up to, Ruf?"

"I got this for Christmas. Trying to talk to an airplane," he replies, still staring at the clouds.

"Ah. That's neat. Good luck!"

Dad comes in the back door and heads straight downstairs to his TV workshop in the corner of the basement (he taught himself TV repair as a side hustle in the early sixties). Which just happens to have a ham radio and a small window with a good, slightly hidden view of the Winkers' backyard. And Rufus. After cracking open a fresh beer, Dad calls me downstairs. And after some dial twirling, he finally latches on to Rufus's frequency and begins a conversation—in the dead-bored, matter-of-fact, jargon-y style of an ex-military airline pilot. "Comin' in loud and clear . . . *KRRCHK* . . . what's your twenty . . . *KRRCHK* . . . TWA eighteen fifty-five . . . *KRRCHK* . . . outbound Wichita . . . *KRRCHK* . . . over . . . *KRRCHK*."

My dad sipping on his beer in the dark with me watching Rufus excitedly running around in circles shouting his name and home address into his handset. Tickled, and trying to contain his own glee, Dad growls at me, "Stop giggling, boy! Now watch this . . . *KRRCHK* . . . Ten-four. Hello, Rufus Winker of Illinois! . . . *KRRCHK* . . . TWA eighteen fifty-five . . . *KRRCHK* . . . We'll be back overhead—inbound at nineteen hundred hours . . . *KRRCHK* . . . gather up some flashlights and shine 'em up at the sky and I'll fly by real low and flash my emergency lights . . . *KRRCHK*."

Seven thirty P.M. CST, casually walking outside with Mom and Dad to ask the Winkers "what the hell are you up to now with them goddamn flashlights?!" Just as their arms were growing heavy and their frustration was starting to boil over, laying bare delicious internal cracks, fissures, and flaws. As they were starting to snipe at each other. Ol' Rufus getting derided from all sides. A veritable schadenfreude buffet.

Might be the closest I ever felt to my mom and dad at the same time. I hate that we bonded over something so mean. I'll take it. But I wish there was more. I hate that there wasn't.

To any surviving Winkers out there, I'd like to say I'm sorry. I'm sure you had your issues, but I'm pretty sure we were the bad guys. In this case at the very least. Love and peace.

13

MY SHARONA

LET'S TALK ABOUT ROCK JOURNALISM FOR A BIT. I like it. I even love some of it. But before I offer up my deeper thoughts on the topic, a caveat directed toward any practitioners of this dark art who might be reading must be stated. Actually, two caveats. I have dual caveats.

First: I'm aware that I am forever indebted to you all for the travail—the shitty pay, the late nights, the stressful deadlines, the long hours. No doubt they have taken their toll on many of you. We share a passion, and without your diligence I'm sure there are countless bands and records I would never have stumbled upon. Thank you.

Second: I'm likewise conscious of the fact that in the grand scheme of things, the bands I've been in and the records I've made, by and large, have been welcomed into the world with a remarkably low level of rancor. Especially considering my reluctance to stop making records and being in bands. There have even been points along the way where I've seen the adorable (and financially chilling) phrase "critics' darling" directed my way. It's been a good run. Nothing I'm about to say should in any way register as complaint.

Okay, one more caveat. (With the caveat that three—now four—caveats is too many caveats. *Yoda voice* Slippery slope, caveats are.) I get that writing about songs and records is technically some form of music journalism we're engaging in here. But I'm really trying to avoid the critic part of that equation (with the exception of Bon Jovi; fuck—another caveat) because that's the problem with music writing; it's the critiquing part, right? The weighing of one against the other, the numbering, the grading, the weird arrogance of forming an opinion, writing it down, and then also giving grades or awarding stars. In effect saying, "Hey, everybody, I wrote a thousand words about the new Crystal Ümlauts LP" (made-up band name) "but if you're in a hurry it's three stars. You know, it's okay, nothing to write home about." It's an odd practice that takes the pretense of writing about art with academic seriousness—dissecting, parsing language, important contextualizing of cultural discourse—then walks it all the way up to the altar and chickens out. "What the hell was I thinking, no one's going to read this shit, ugh . . . here, here's a number, it means it's pretty good. You like music? Well, this is music. It's . . . okay."

I guess it makes sense that music journalism has a tough time getting its story straight about how seriously it wants to be taken. Because let's face it, the idea that what makes music so important at its core could be critiqued and rated is laughable in the face of the genuine promise almost any record can deliver to the listener. A promise that says, "I am here. Sing with me. Out loud or to yourself. I will always be here when you need me, you are not alone." Songs are our companions. Some become friends for life, but any song in the air has the potential to keep you company for a little while. The way you might form a brief bond with someone in the checkout line. Rock 'n' roll is doubly insulated from the indignities of being assayed by the mind alone. By my definition, rock 'n' roll is anything that can be itself without thinking or fear of consequence. Best friend material in my book. It's music made by bored teenagers, maladjusted adults, and most important, inspired amateurs.

Great rock 'n' roll can be, and often is, much better than the people making it. A lot of times it happens in spite of the contrivances surrounding its genesis. It's magic that can be conjured almost anywhere by almost anyone. Because we as listeners get a say, too. We can make something truly rock 'n' roll just by hearing it with a pure heart. There's no point in arguing about it. Which is why it was so confusing for me as a kid to see so much critical vitriol heaped on the Knack's first record. Not that they weren't right in the long run. The band did have reprehensible lyrics. There were contrivances. But boy did that shit sound stupid when "My Sharona" came on the radio. Totally undeniable rock miracle. It stirred something in me in 1979 that has yet to come to rest.

At twelve years old, I didn't have a lot of friends who could hang with my obsessive level of rock zealotry. So again, as we've seen in previous chapters, that left only my mom to talk to. Fortunately for me, she was able to be a genuinely patient and indulging listener. She'd smile and nod. Obviously bemused to see her often withdrawn and quiet kid enthusiastic about anything.

So we're in the drive-thru at McDonald's. I'd already heard "My Sharona" a few times by now. And as I was getting worked up trying to explain how great it was to my mom, it came on the radio. Unbelievable timing. Now, for those of you who don't remember, there were two versions—one was a radio edit for the shorter song format of AM pop radio, and then there was the longer album version that the more freewheeling FM stations would play. I was so excited that we were listening to KSHE, because that meant that the extended middle section of the song would be intact. The part of the song I had just breathlessly proclaimed to my mother to be the hardest of all the rocking I had ever heard. Pointing out that the rocking gets so hard and strenuous that at one point you can actually hear the musicians breathing heavily.

"Oh wow," she says as we pull up to the pickup

window. "Here it is!" I say as I crank the volume. Now my mother is reaching to grab a bag containing my Filet-O-Fish and fries from a frightened cashier as Doug Fieger climaxes to the beat blowing out the dash speakers of my mom's Caprice Classic. As we slowly move back into traffic, she calmly rolls her window back up and turns the radio down. The color of her face foreshadowing the lessons of a health class unit I had heard about but had yet to be taught. And I arrived at the conclusion that I would prefer to always think of the panting-and-heaving section of "My Sharona" the way I had originally interpreted it.

IN GERMANY BEFORE
THE WAR

IT'S HARD TO BELIEVE A SONG LIKE THIS COULD POS-
sibly coexist on the same album with a song like "Short
People." Much less on the same side—but there they are,
bookending side one on Randy Newman's 1977 album
Little Criminals. Wanna know something else hard to
believe? "Short People" was a massive hit. It would have
even made it to number one on the *Billboard* charts if it
weren't for "Baby Come Back" by Player. Oh, that and
another little song called "STAYIN' ALIVE" by the Bee
Gees. I'm guessing number two still feels pretty great,
though, when the song above yours is a cultural phe-
nomenon, not to mention an unstoppable juggernaut of
record sales.

I, like most people, bought *Little Criminals* for "Short
People." Which at the time was sort of controversial. Because a lot of people were dumb and couldn't understand the idea that a singer could sing something they

themselves didn't believe. I knew it was a song about prejudice, and I was ten. It wasn't Randy Newman's fault people were laughing at the wrong joke, but I'm sure it sucked to be a little person in 1978 when this song was a close-to-unavoidable part of daily life. This is the kind of thing people like to point to and say stuff like, "There's no way you could get away with a song like that today," and usually I think to myself that they're being small-minded dopes.

But in this case, I think they have a point. Randy Newman himself would probably think better of rolling the dice with a song as mean-spirited as this one today. You can tell people all day long that your lyrics are sung from the point of view of an untrustworthy narrator, and these days I think it's just going to make them angrier.

So things change. Good. But if it weren't for this nasty pop anomaly I wouldn't have been exposed to "In Germany Before the War" at the perfect time in my life to scare me out of my wits, and at the same time light my imagination on fire by exposing me to the wild mood-shaping power of chord voicing and orchestral arranging. This song represents the first glimmer my young mind ever perceived of the true scope of what just the music part of a song can do—how truly infinite the realm of possibilities is tonally. I still know of no better song to illustrate how clearly the text of a song can be illuminated by its musical habitat. We are never told explicitly what happens to the "little girl" who "lost her way." The music alone conveys that horror. Leaves no doubt. Is this song for everybody? No. It's not a song I would throw on at a BBQ. But it is special to me. Which is the point of this book. Sharing how songs big and small, funny and dark, consoling AND upsetting, all end up rattling around in the same head is, to me, fascinating beyond compare and worthy of some book-length introspection.

I'm also amazed at how funny it is, at least in my opinion, that this song exists in the same universe as "Short People," much less on the same album. A hit single, mind you, the seven-inch of which came in a sleeve that admonished purchasers to keep it stored on a high shelf out of reach of . . . um, you get it. Can you imagine?! So there's that. But "In Germany Before the War" really is a masterpiece of musical storytelling. And I do think about it often when I'm trying to get a recording I'm working on to tell the listener where to look when the words alone can't. When I'm trying my best to get people to look at the river but think of the sea, as the chorus of this song says. A simple couplet that somehow perfectly captures the dissociation of a serial killer and at the same time tells you exactly how music works. How an illusion can be built upon the genuine discomfort of a major melody over a minor chord.

Randy Newman tells us what to look at by showing us what isn't there. With music. I'm still striving to learn how to conjure that type of magic. I want to make things that make people feel and know things without any thinking on their part. It's kind of the whole point. It's why it's so unimportant to dwell upon what songs "mean." If you could just tell someone a melody, music wouldn't be necessary. I might not have understood it at the time I first heard this song, but this is the song I still turn to the most to relearn this beautiful truth about what it is that I aspire to do.

THE UN-COPIED COPY

DUPLICATING UNCLE TUPELO'S FIRST DEMO TAPE ONE at a time on a dual cassette deck from Sears.

Cutting out and folding the hand-drawn xeroxed cardboard "J-cards" and inserting them into the ridiculously fragile and unnervingly sharp plastic cassette cases.

Remembering the specific kind of cuticle damage loading cassette cases would inevitably cause.

All of these steps feeling like a leap forward into the modern world of efficiency and automation compared to our previous process.

Which in the past was, when a bar owner or club booker would ask, "Do you have a demo tape?" we would tense up and nod. Then we would solemnly trudge back to whoever's basement we were practicing in at the time. Press record on a cheap boom box and record ourselves playing the four or five songs we considered our "best" . . .

say, "Psycho" by the Sonics, "Hang on Sloopy" (the Remains version), "Are You Gonna Be There (At the Love-In)" by the Chocolate Watchband, and, um . . . "Louie Louie" probably. Press eject, write the name of the band and our phone numbers on the commercially provided track card, and then drive the one and only copy directly back to the bar or club we were hoping would give us a gig. For every bar or club, that's what we did—we'd hand over the only copy. The un-copied copy. For years. It never occurred to us that we could duplicate a cassette until one of us asked why some boom boxes have places for two tapes.

Part of being the bass player in those days meant you were the one responsible for a lot of legwork. Scrounging up gigs, going to Kinko's, flyer-ing telephone poles, etc.

Name the three pieces of gear every bass player needs.

A bass, an amp . . . and a staple gun.

That's how the joke used to go.

DANCING QUEEN

IT'S IMPORTANT IN LIFE TO ADMIT WHEN YOU WERE wrong about something. And although I bristle at the notion that there could ever be such a thing as a "wrong" musical opinion, I was relieved when I finally was able to admit I was colossally wrong about this song (and ABBA in general). I'm happy I can admit it. Maybe even a touch proud of myself for not digging my heels in and hating this song for even a second longer than I had to, unlike some friends I know who are still holding out. To me the weird part is ever feeling like I had to hate something so clearly irresistible.

At the time this song came out there were very strict lines in the sand being drawn between cultural camps. This tune was located deep in "enemy" territory, at the intersection of pop and disco. I personally liked pop radio because occasionally a gem would slip through the cracks. You'd get a "Saturday Night" by the Bay City

Rollers or "You're My Best Friend" by Queen. Or something absurd like "Convoy" would make it on the Top 40 and brighten your day. I was just self-possessed enough as a nine-year-old in 1976 to be able to see how overblown my brother's lectures on the dangers of "bubblegum" music were. So I could tune him out when he'd go on about how my "brain was still developing" and I "must be vigilant against IQ-lowering aspects of TV and pop culture."

But disco was despised by practically everyone I knew (with the exception of the kids who liked to roller skate; that seemed to be where the line was drawn). Basically, meaning that to all of the males older than myself in my extended family sphere, disco had taken on the profile of something legitimately wrong. A world-destroying force that we must all unite against. So it was easy at the time to say, "Okay, I'm not even going to listen to that music because that music SUCKS!" And of course, there was also the additional specter of an added adjective—disco was "gay." And to nine-year-old boys who didn't know any better, *gay* meant "bad." Really bad. And to my teenage cousins wrestling with a bit of sexual ambiguity, *gay* was really scary and really bad. And tragically, even to almost all of the adults I knew, who definitely should have known better, *gay* was bad. Where I grew up, when I grew up, just saying you liked something that had been deemed "gay" meant YOU were gay. It was no joke. Add to this the fact that, musically, disco was a technology-embracing extension of Black American musical forms and, as a movement, seemed to be utterly ignoring the traditional American Black/white racial divide . . . and, well, that's just too much ignorance for even the most confident child (which I was not) to sort through and reject.

I wish I could say that looking back on that time from 2023 makes it hard to believe people were ever so small-minded and bigoted. But of course it's entirely believable because *I'm waving my arms around*.

I'm taking a moment here to make clear to you, the reader, that I do understand the band I'm talking about here was/is white (Swedish! Sooo white!) and straight. It doesn't matter. Or at least it didn't matter at the time, because it was "disco." It was thoroughly demonized, and for all the wrong reasons.

And so through all of the societal forces at play and by my own weakness, I never allowed myself to like it. Until years later, after I'd already started trying to write songs and found myself staring at an overhead speaker in a grocery store aisle (not stoned!) just reeling at this familiar melody and how exuberantly sad it was. "Having the time of your life!" A real come-to-Jesus moment. A real come–to–Agnetha, Björn, Benny, and Anni-Frid moment.

But before that day, I, along with many others, had denied myself undeniable joy. Countless fantastic records and deep grooves were dismissed and derided out of ignorance. Of course, this song and this music was always going to win eventually. Because it's just too special to ignore forever.

There are wrong opinions about music! And to this day, "Dancing Queen" is the song I always think of when I THINK I don't like something. It taught me that I can't ever completely trust my negative reactions. I was burned so badly by this one song being withheld from my heart for so long. I try to never listen to music without first politely asking my mind, and whatever blind spots I'm afflicted with today, to move aside long enough for my gut to be the judge. And even then, if I don't like something I make a mental note to try again in ten years.

Melodies as pure and evocative as the one in "Dancing Queen" don't come along every day. I'm sad for every single moment I missed loving this song. Playing it again right now. Making up for lost spins. I truly recommend spending some time looking for a song you might have unfairly maligned. It feels good to stop hating something. Music is a good place to start if you're interested in forgiveness. For yourself, mostly, I assume. Because records can't really change much over time, but we sure can, and do. Better late than never.

THE MESSAGE

WHAT GENRE OF MUSIC'S BIRTH DO YOU THINK I FEEL the most connected to? Wrong. It's not alt-country. Guess again . . . wrong!

Okay, I'll give you a hint. It's hip-hop. The answer is hip-hop. And that's because I was at the right age during the right moment in history to witness the mind-blowing birth of a new genre. No, I wasn't there at the block parties in the Bronx when turntables transformed into expressive instruments and, along with samplers and drum machines, razed the playing field so level anyone with something to say could now, in fact, get that shit off of their chest.

However, I was there shortly after. Along with practically everyone else alive at the time not living under a rock, I got to be among the first humans to buy a "rap" record. Sugarhill Gang's "Rapper's Delight." And again, it wasn't like I was some twelve-year-old musical adventurer out there alone, blazing a trail with less worldly listeners lagging behind. No. This song was instantly everywhere. Kids I knew who never seemed to show interest in music of any kind were walking around singing "Rock it out baby bubba to the boogity bang bang the boogie to the boogie the beat."

It was exciting beyond belief. The racial divides that generally ruled Top 40 radio (an issue that sadly persists to this day) seemed to disappear for a brief and glorious stretch of time in the late seventies and, to a lesser degree, into the early eighties. Next it was Kurtis Blow's "The Breaks" for me. Which is not as talked about these days. I would imagine I knew the track was due to Kurtis being from the St. Louis area, rather than any indication of or argument for the legitimacy of my status as an "OG." Blondie's "Rapture" technically had some "rapping" on it. Pretty bad "rapping" that, by today's standards, kind of sounds like my margarita-buzzed sister "spitting rhymes" at brunch—"a man from mars / eating cars / going to bars / what the heck / I'll pick up the check"— but I'll accept it. Very cool of them to give it a go.

But the moment that really hammered home the fact that this music was not just some pop music anomaly— a gimmick that would fizzle out once it fell out of fashion, like the wah-wah pedal or yodeling—was when "The Message" by Grandmaster Flash and the Furious Five hit the airwaves and kicked everyone's ass into gear. This was the moment where it became clear that hip-hop was a vitally important whole new form of musical expression. Even a dumb kid like myself could hear it when this song came on the radio. Dylan never wrote anything nearly as incisive and direct. "The answer, my friend, is blowin' in the wind" sounds pretty much like a greeting card next to

> People pissing on the stairs you know they just don't
>   care . . .
> Don't push me 'cause I'm close to the edge
> I'm trying not to lose my head

"The Message" is a carved-in-stone moment for me. Every verse is instantly accessible in my memory. I've come to think of this as a type of high-art journalism. Like Woody Guthrie. This is front-lines war correspondence the way the ancients did it. Setting the scene of what it was like to survive the inner-city deprivations of the late seventies and early eighties to a sturdy hypnotic poem, and then sending it out across oceans of time and space with the understanding that being a witness to suffering demands documentation. Haters gonna hate. But witnesses gonna witness. And art gets the last word.

OVERDUBS

LATE AT NIGHT, HELPING SOME FRIENDS (ALSO IN their teens) record their band at a studio in downtown Belleville. Going slow.

Scary-looking biker dude busts in the front door furiously looking for Dave, the guy who owns the studio and is "producing" the session.

Finds Dave under the mixing desk. Drags Dave into the tracking room by his mullet and gives him a merciless beating as we all steer clear in stunned silence. At one point, I swear he played my friend's drums with Dave's head.

Tired and apparently satisfied with the punishment he's delivered, the low-rent Terminator leaves.

Dave, acting as if this is part of his daily routine, pops up off the floor. Bleeding from his mouth and with one eye swollen shut, he asks cheerfully, "Where were we? Overdubs?"

BALANCING ACT

WHEN YOU'RE AN ANGSTY KID, YOU'RE AN EASY mark for angsty songs. It's hard to avoid the very specific, painfully earnest spectacle of asking a parent or love interest or pet to sit down and listen to a record that somehow expresses "exactly" how you feel.

Speaking for myself, these embarrassing scenes from my teenage years most typically were played out at our yellow Formica kitchen table with my mom squinting at me through cigarette smoke, speakers aimed down the stairs from my attic bedroom, my gaze averted, mouthing the words, occasionally lifting my eyes toward my mother's patient and neutral face, trying to gauge whether or not she was "getting it."

For the life of me, I can't figure out why describing this tableau still fills me with something approaching shame. Maybe I'm still worried that letting on about the degree to which I was emotionally dependent upon my mother makes me "less than." Or I suppose it's possible that I'm still feeling a vestigial sense of guilt about the level of indulgence and support I enjoyed at home, when even at the time I was aware of how rare that truly is. Like the urge to conceal an extravagant gift around friends having a tougher time scraping by.

But in reality, I think that what once looked self-flatteringly poignant and unique has been revealed by time to be pretty par for the course. The course being adolescence, naturally. So while the attempt to be better understood by asking someone to look at us through the lens of someone else's song fits the outlines we're all busy trying to color in at "that" age, I will say I'm not sure the songs I was picking as surrogates got much airplay outside of our kitchen. Whenever I think of this song by the Volcano Suns, it feels frozen forever in the amber of my youth. Suspended in the air surrounding my mother's mind striving to understand her sad son's alienation. Head cocked sincerely, leaning into the words. Nodding and tearing up at the tears falling from my cheeks.

How should I act in a crowd?
Should I voice my feelings
For acquaintances?
Should I feel lucky to be a part of the wheeling and
    dealing no matter what is said?
. . . It matters, it matters, it MATTERS TO ME!

I'm glad this song was there for me. It still means a lot to me. It's hard when you feel so many things so deeply. It's even harder when you care a lot and the world keeps not giving a shit.

It still matters to me, and I couldn't have said it better myself.

FRANKIE TEARDROP

IN 1982 BRUCE SPRINGSTEEN PUT OUT A STARK HOME-recorded acoustic album called *Nebraska*. The bulk of the songs put the singer's voice squarely behind the wheel of a car, narrating tales of desperation and redemption. From both sides of the law. It's a desolate record. Beautifully rendered, unmistakably American landscapes place it alongside the short stories of Flannery O'Connor, Capote's *In Cold Blood*, and our sick romanticizing of Charles Starkweather's real-life murder spree. These are all influences directly cited at the time by the Boss himself. And to Bruce's credit, he also made a point of professing his admiration of and his indebtedness to a band little known to most of his audience: Suicide.

I'll be honest, I felt pretty proud of myself for noticing the connection before I heard Mr. Springsteen fess up to the inspiration. Suicide was a band on my radar through sheer luck and good fortune, thanks to the previously discussed odd programming choices of *The Midnight Special*'s "New Wave" episode. But it wasn't like it required a truly sophisticated ear to hear that the vocal tics and lyrical phrasing on *Nebraska* were directly lifted from Suicide's singer, Alan Vega. It was obvious, but only if you'd ever heard Suicide. Which made me cool because, again, not a lot of people had at the time. Plus, I was probably in the running to be considered among the youngest of all the people on the planet (or at least in my hometown) who could claim awareness of said protopunk band, Suicide. First band to call themselves punk, by the way—in 1970, no less!

Now, with all due respect to Bruce, there's a big difference between the real deal and a loving homage. And while Bruce's portrayal of the desolation of the American psyche is nuanced and convincing in an actorly way, when you hear something like the Suicide song "Frankie Teardrop," it makes Bruce sound like John Denver. It still stands at the limit of the amount of torment and terror that can be captured on a recording. *Nebraska*'s characters sound like they come from a modern western— beautifully lit, acted out on blacktop in bucket seats. Serious and moralistic. Good art. What Alan Vega is doing, on the other hand, is hard to fathom. No one in their right mind would want to go where he's determined to take us. It sounds like he doesn't have a choice. And if he has to listen to the sound of a murdered murderer's tortured screams from the depths of hell breaking apart his brain, it's only fair he gets to claw at us from the grave.

Seriously, though. Don't listen to this track if you aren't in the mood to be legitimately upset. Also, pro parenting tip—don't cue this song up on a dark country road for your young teenage child driving them home from an aborted sleepover gone bad. I know someone who did that (me) and nearly a decade later it still comes up when my parental judgment is in question.

SEVENTIES
CAPRICE CLASSIC

ONE A.M., MAKING THE DECISION TO ABANDON MY seventies Caprice Classic after nearly an hour of struggling, pushing, gunning, turning tires, spinning tires, rocking, don't forget to rock it . . . trying to get myself unstuck from the fucking ice and snow—excuse me, "wintry mix"—in an alley behind a friend's apartment in the Soulard Market area of St. Louis.

Figuring I should remove the license plates to avoid being fined for illegal dumping or whatnot.

Desperately fumbling at the rusty screws with my bare, frozen fingers. Giving up. Then, Hulk-like, furiously folding and unfolding and yanking at the virtually indestructible aluminum alloy the state of Illinois made license plates out of. Finally tearing off the weakened tags. Triumph!

Burying the mangled shards of my Illinois license

plates in the snow. Behind some trash cans. Just to be safe.

Have I mentioned this happened before I quit drinking?

No? Okay. Well, I'm pretty sure I had been drinking on this particular evening.

So, I guess the plan was . . .

Um . . . I'm not sure if I understand what "the plan" was, even now.

I suppose I was tired and drunk and I had no way to call a tow truck. And/or I was too dumb to think of a more responsible plan. Even the thought of asking a friend to help seems to have slipped my mind. I guess because it would have involved walking a few blocks each way in the bitter cold.

Actually, it just came to me. The plan was, I wanted to go to sleep. Like, right away. If the car was there in the morning, then I'd have a clearer head (as if) to deal with it. Or . . . maybe all of the snow and ice would melt?

And if it wasn't there?

Spoiler alert: It was not. I assume it was towed by the city of St. Louis to some impound lot. I never followed up because I was afraid I'd get slapped with a fine. And in those days there was a very real chance a municipal fine might actually exceed the three hundred or so dollars I had invested in this bald-tired bucket of rusting American steel.

So I had no car. I didn't deserve to have a car.

And I think that's the judgment I made at the moment I committed to ditching the car.

I think about this episode of my life most often when I'm watching some true-crime documentary. Where after hours and hours of interrogation a couple of belligerent cops get some scared kid to falsely confess to murdering his whole family.

Most of the time the problem is that they're all just tired and want to go home. I have empathy for all parties. The cops don't have a clue and have wasted too much time already talking to an innocent kid to even begin to stomach the idea of having to start all over with some new lead.

And the kid? Well, there but for the grace of you-know-who go I.

Because I learned a couple of things about myself in that alley that night.

1. I would absolutely admit to murdering anyone and anything if the promise of getting to go home and go to sleep were being dangled as the carrot.

2. I would absolutely murder and bury a license plate if a hopelessly ice-mired car stood between me and a bed.

I'M NOT IN LOVE

ONE OF THE AMAZING THINGS SONGS CAN DO IN the mind of a single listener is transform, over time, from something reviled and loathed to the point of avoidance—an instant radio-dial-lunge type of track— to something breathtakingly beautiful and essential.

Take this song, by 10cc, for example. When this song came out, I hated it so much I actually kind of feared it. There was something about the middle section that made me feel "super icky," as I would have put it at the time. The part where it sounds like you're coming out of a coma, stuck inside your body, unable to move or communicate but aware of the people whispering around your hospital bed—that part really bothered me, and describing it now, I must admit, has reawakened some vestigial anxiety I was in the process of claiming to have transcended.

But that doesn't change the fact that this song, over time, went from Brussels sprouts to cake in my ears' taste buds, somehow. Or I guess, more accurately, it went from my eight-year-old opinion of Brussels sprouts to my current grown-ass status as a person who can't get enough of those odd roll-y little balls of plant stuff.

So yeah, I'm basically just saying our tastes change. What we want from a song can evolve. And again, the song itself obviously doesn't change. We do. We notice and appreciate things we missed. In the case of this track, it's not surprising that a kid, unschooled and uninterested in the ways of love, might miss the pitch-black dark humor of the lyric

> I keep your picture upon the wall
> It hides a nasty stain that's lying there
> So don't you ask me to give it back
> I know you know it doesn't mean that much to me

That line alone might have warranted a reevaluation. But the thing that kills me now when I hear this song is how masterfully conceived it is. From the arrangement to the tonal textures chosen, this recording creates its own internal logic. A feat of engineering few songs ever come close to. It sounds like no other song on earth, an alien-sounding song about alienation, and at the same time it was so successful at drawing people in that it became a massive hit. Otherwise, I wouldn't have heard it as a kid and then kept bumping into it on the radio the rest of my life until it wound up in this book. Where I'm telling you how great it is.

CONNECTION

I HAVE A TON OF FAVORITE RECORDS. A LOT OF THEM are records that had already withstood the test of time well before they ever landed on my turntable. Your Beatles, your Dylans, your Supremes, your Ronettes . . . you know, your basic wide-swath pop-rock-centric canon. Maybe an equal number to that are records that I got to buy firsthand (punk era onward through the indie years to today) or albums I discovered as reissues of lesser-known artists—records that people would pretend they already knew but were really new to most of us. Records that deserved an audience and finally found one among my generation of record freaks (things like Os Mutantes and Karen Dalton come to mind).

And then there are a handful of records that feel like I'm the only one in the world who cares about them. Records that make you feel the urge to evangelize. I know that it's unlikely there could truly be any publicly released music that found its way to my heart alone. But some records really get overlooked, and it's strange when you realize a record that's become a constant companion reliably draws blank stares when brought up. Even with your biggest music-snob pals.

Now, occasionally you really do fall in love with something that comes by its obscurity the old-fashioned way—by being extremely rare in terms of the number manufactured and its nearly nonexistent commercial appeal. Those are the records that get buffed like badges at the counters of indie record stores—"What?! You've never heard Plaid Turd? Oh man. Their first EP is easily in my top five all-time crap-core slabs." I do believe there's a certain amount of pity warranted toward a person who would state something like that.

But it should also be noted that, no. No it isn't. The person saying this is not telling the truth. Plaid Turd, good as they may be (I just made them up), are not favorite-record material. That poor nerd has built an identity around records. More specifically, they're the kind of person who has little to no self-esteem outside of the extremely niche body of knowledge some maladaptive obsession has bestowed upon them. People who act like the farther an artist is away from having an actual audience is a reliable measure of musical worth. You know who I'm talking about. And you know who you are. I see myself in you. My judgment is harsh but fair. Self-examination has revealed these truths.

But that's not what I'm here to talk about. I'm more fascinated by the lesser-known or even deeply maligned works of artists that are otherwise highly considered. And how I think it's cool that a record like *Between the Buttons* by the Rolling Stones can achieve a cherished status based on a few unlikely twists of fate. Like how in my house growing up, a very high percentage of the records we owned were purchased from bargain bins. Cutouts—records marked for clearance by having a triangular piece of the album jacket's upper right-hand corner cut out or similarly defaced. If it weren't for cutouts, I doubt my older siblings would have ever been allowed to buy a Stones record. By the time I came around, they had all mostly left home, but their records remained. So my favorite Stones record is the one no one gave a shit about when I was growing up. I know that now it's regarded as a classic, but I still rarely see it mentioned alongside the more commonly accepted Stones canon. Mick Jagger himself has described *Between the Buttons* as "more or less rubbish."

Well, I think Mr. Jagger's opinion is rubbish. Because this shit slaps. (Am I saying that right?)

Listen to "Connection." I've been trying to write my version of "Connection" for about forty years. It's in my DNA. My favorite song on my favorite Stones album. All because a record company miscalculated and overshot an already ridiculously high demand just enough for it to end up discounted and thus fit my folks' meager budget.

TRAUMATIZING TOILET

FOR YEARS I THOUGHT THAT MY MIND HAD SIMPLY enhanced or possibly even fabricated the utterly traumatizing toilet at CBGB's. Could it have possibly been in the open on a riser in the corner of the room? With no WALLS?!

Yes. Yes, that's exactly how it was. An installation at the Met and photos confirm it. And yes—I was scarred for life by the absolute necessity to employ this facility.

FOREVER PARADISE

IN THE LATE SEVENTIES THE UNDERTONES WERE thought of as the Irish Ramones. Checks out. Their members came from places with names like Bogside and Creggan. They formed in Derry. And if you've ever listened to their first record, you know the Ramones inspiration is an undeniable shoe that fits. They were a great band. Bright, tuneful three-chord punk rock. Catchy melodies. Nowhere near as lyrically demented as their New York counterparts, but still in the general ballpark of the Ramones.

A lot of classic angsty pop subject matter. Boy/girl troubles. Girl/boy/other boy troubles. Not much about "the Troubles" troubles, but who can blame them for craving a little escape. It was energetic kid stuff. Wildly effective, simple broken-heart cures in the form of two-minute-thirty-second blasts of bummed-out joy. They had the hooks for hits, too. In the UK they got on the charts with their first single, "Teenage Kicks." It didn't go to number one, but before he died the legendary BBC DJ John Peel did claim it was his all-time favorite song. They did crack the top ten in the UK with a single off of their second record, the utterly charming "My Perfect Cousin."

In the States nothing ever really got going for them. I knew about them because I used to read the imported British rock tabloids (*NME, Melody Maker, Sounds*) cover to cover at my local record store. Occasionally, I'd buy an issue just to re-up the record clerks' tolerance of my loitering. The music press in the UK was incredibly fickle. They fully embraced the role of tabloid journalism. The pressure to sell a new issue every week— find new bands, create new sensations, generate fashion crazes—made them insane. They made it sound like the British bands were reinventing the concept of music hourly.

At some point I figured out the fever pitch of excitement surrounding every new band they championed was a bit of a scam. I think it was reading a headline calling the band Haircut 100 "exciting" with a cover photo of six guys with cable-knit sweaters tied over their shoulders, James Spader–style, that finally allowed the penny to drop on what was really going on with these mags.

But once again, I have to acknowledge the good with the bad. Because the Undertones went on to make one of my favorite albums of all time. These sleazy rags with their questionable motives hipped me to the Undertones. And by the time they were no longer the hot new band gracing their covers, I happened to still care about them enough to buy their third album, *Positive Touch*. I also liked their second album, *Hypnotised*. Similar to their first lyrically, but musically searching and hinting at a sophistication far beyond the three-chord structures of their debut. But nothing could have prepared me for the quantum leap that *Positive Touch* represented when it came out in 1981.

Positive Touch has been my constant companion since then, even though it quickly disappeared from even the UK charts, never mind never making the US charts. I can think of no other pop record quite like it. I'm always inspired by the inventiveness of its arrangements. Bands are human-scale miracles. Any band that sounds good playing together has created magic. But when a band throws away a formula as sturdy and true as the one the Undertones were so good at, and believes in themselves and each other enough to find a way to sound like only themselves—to create a music that exists only because they looked for it somewhere inside of themselves—knowing that there's a record they want to hear and that the only way they'll ever get to hear it is to make it themselves . . . Well, that's a miracle made of miracles.

"Forever Paradise" is the last song on side two. The

preferred last song of the evening on school nights. It's a bit eerie. Piano notes sleepwalking into the mist. Beautiful androgynous vocal. Fractures into an extended backward sound collage that puts itself together again for the last chorus:

Forever and ever
Forever and ever
Forever and ever
Forever and ever
Paradise

My dreams often play this song in the background.

At a time in my life when everything felt like forever but not much resembled paradise, this song was a comfort. And falling asleep to it was as perfectly content as I ever got in those days.

SATAN, YOUR KINGDOM MUST COME DOWN

HAVE YOU EVER HEARD OF A MAN NAMED JOHN CO-
hen? Whether you have or haven't, it's probably safe to
say you're unaware of the outsize role he played in shaping the impression Uncle Tupelo made on the world. He,
along with Harry Smith and his *Anthology of American
Folk Music*, was among the very first to open a window
into our country's musical past and say, "Hey, get a load
of how wild this stuff is!" The band he formed with some
fellow travelers in the late fifties to document and perform old-time folk tunes, the New Lost City Ramblers,
and the albums they recorded, is where Jay Farrar and I
first heard the Carter Family song "No Depression." In
fact, it was only much later, after naming our debut album *No Depression* and performing the song for years,
that we finally got to hear the Carters' original recording,
the one that the New Lost City Ramblers had learned the
song from.

So right there a big chunk of what Uncle Tupelo is known for wouldn't have happened without our hero John Cohen. If you have the time, you really should look him up and marvel at his accomplishments. But the thing he did that most changed my life was travel around the rural South and collect songs. He wasn't the only person doing this, of course. I cherish his work alongside that of John and Alan Lomax and many other folklorists and musicologists. Their belief in the world-shaping power of song has, no doubt, led me here to this book. Admittedly, my work here is much more internal and less academic in its conception, but I do believe I'm guided by a similar passion to share not just songs but their ability to get up and walk around and form new landscapes as they travel.

To be specific about John Cohen's contribution to our recorded history, I'd like to point you in the direction of *High Atmosphere: Ballads and Banjo Tunes from Virginia and North Carolina*, a collection of field recordings done by John circa 1965 and subsequently released in 1975 on Rounder Records.

Just a side note on how hard it was to get your hands on archival folk recordings like these by the time the mideighties rolled around. "Out of print" usually meant "good luck ever even seeing a copy." Your best shot at owning a title like *High Atmosphere* was to check it out from a local library and never return it. Which is something I would never do (but I knew a guy who would).

My copy of *High Atmosphere* was legit, though. I found it in the used bins. It was a fluke. The type of lucky find that for Jay Farrar and me would lead to deep resentment in the heart of the party fortune had frowned upon. Resulting in whispered arguments, side by side, no eye contact, still dutifully flipping through the racks—"No! I'm not letting you buy it! I'll let you tape it! It's not my fault you started in the M's."

Uncle Tupelo recorded three songs we had learned off of this same album, including the one we're about to discuss—"Satan, Your Kingdom Must Come Down." It's a very old-sounding song sung by a very old-sounding man named Frank Proffitt. The premise is, you got it, Satan's kingdom must, you know, come down.

How we go about making that happen changes as the song progresses. First, we're going to pray. If that doesn't work (spoiler: it won't), we'll sing. Still no luck? Then we're going to have to shout. "Shout until they tear your kingdom down." So the question is, why would this nonbeliever (me, not Frank. Frank is a believer without a doubt) find this song so utterly compelling and cathartic? So much so that I wanted to sing it myself. Why did I believe I could sing this song convincingly? I think it was something about how old it all felt. How clearly it made the struggle to deal with all the bullshit an eternal ordeal. This song and performance helped me form a connection to the angst of the past. It's silly sounding, perhaps, but, god, did it feel good to know that the crappy way I felt wasn't new. Granted, this isn't what most people would ever get out of this song. Surely I was projecting at IMAX proportions. But I still feel it. And I stand by my interpretation's validity.

Because what I was really searching for in those days was authenticity. I craved it. There was a deep need to feel like I wasn't always being lied to. That there were, in fact, "real" things in the world. Not everything was an agreed-upon fiction like the flag, or dollar bills, or sports "teams."

Or, of course, the shared delusions of religion. Punk rock records gave me a lot of hope, but they weren't foolproof. Bands could burn you by "selling out." Which is kind of a quaint concept these days. It was dumb. But it really did hurt at the time.

So recordings like this—where one isn't even sure the person singing understands that they're being recorded, and, let's face it, by now they're almost certainly dead—became the gold standard for authenticity in our world. This music was unassailably pure. The fact that this song refers to Satan, one of the top three hallucinations of all time, made not one bit of difference. What I heard then, and what I still hear today, is what I always thought was written in the margins of punk music. The defiant dream that for good to triumph over every fucking thing in the world that sucks, all of the evil, all of the greed, all of the phoniness, all of it, everything you hate—all you have to do is keep singing.

Don't stop. Shout if you have to. Whatever you think "Satan's kingdom" might be, however strong a hold you might think the "devils" have on the world, it's no match for a teenager in their bedroom listening to a broken voice and a rattling banjo echoing some truth through the trees.

BROWN RECLUSE
SPIDER BITE

REMEMBERING THE TOUR BUS DRIVER WHO SHOWED up in Chicago along with his wife. Our road manager at the time said, "We only hired you." Bus driver, pulling back his coat, revealing a gun at his hip. He said, "She's comin' along. 'Cause I gotta brown recluse spider bite on my leg, and she's gonna help keep it clean."

Waking up at the hotel one morning and realizing the bus, and all of our gear, was gone. Asking where they'd been when they returned two days later, only to hear that they'd been "visitin' friends."

Surprised to find out, in the middle of the night, that the wife was driving, and the husband was sleeping. Our road manager asked them to pull over and switch drivers, and she said, "That's fine, I was done with my shift anyway." She pulled into a truck stop and bought some hard lemonade. At this point, our nerves were wrecked, so a lot of us were in the front lounge, not sleeping, listening through the curtain to what they were doing. He was driving now, and she was drinking. I heard her say, "You want one?" and he said, "I'll have a swaller." And she poured it into his coffee mug.

Back in those days, we couldn't do anything about much, because we'd get stranded. We weren't high on the list with the bus companies.

GOD DAMN JOB

UP UNTIL NOW I'VE BEEN WRITING ABOUT RECORDED
music, primarily. Aside from thinking my cousin wrote
"Takin' Care of Business," all of the previous chapters
have been about songs that exist as records. You can
cross-reference them—maybe hear them for the first
time, or see if they hit your ears any different after reading about them. It's safe to assume most of these songs
are accessible through the wonders of modern technology, and accessible without a whole lot of trouble. If
I tell you I had some type of life-shaping spiritual event
listening to, let's say, ELO's "Telephone Line," you can
go hear for yourself and test whether or not that magic
works on you as well.

This song, however, is different. Even though there is
a record to reference, a record that I own, purchased the
following day after the event I'm about to describe, this
song is one I first heard live, and it was delivered to me

like a punch to the chest. Viscerally. I can still feel it. It was a once-in-a-lifetime moment. Something I witnessed with my own eyes and ears, even though now it only exists inside me as a memory. A crazy, cherished memory. The kind of memory that ends up sounding both overblown and pale when stated out loud, like pointing at a ghost no one else can see.

But to me, this moment was so . . . um, momentous, that it feels like it could take the rest of this book to put it into the proper perspective. Or maybe it's more like trying to convince you that I once saw lightning strike a duck or that I was walking around a hotel lobby hungry one time and a vending machine I glanced at longingly spontaneously began spitting out snacks at my feet. Just one of those slices of life that, when recounted, gets one's mundane mixed up in one's fantasy and one's fantasy mixed up in one's mundane. A precarious tale to tell—I picture you nodding off, the way I drift away when someone tries to tell me about the dream they had last night. "Wow, that's crazy," I interject as I give up on trying to form a corollary mental picture. Point is, it's nearly impossible to get these moments pinned down in writing with any shape resembling a true epiphany. Because the part that's missing—the part that can't ever be completely conveyed—is you (or me in this instance . . . er, you know what I mean). And how the stage these pivotal scenes are acted out on is set against a vast internal backdrop no one else has enough mental energy (or mind paint, to further the metaphor) to complete.

So I'm going to ask you to help me out a little. Please. If you don't mind. Try to picture a moment from your youth when you felt empty—weary beyond your years, bored with everything, including yourself. Maybe even more than a little bit sad for no real reason. Did you ever feel like that? I have not met many people who can't relate, but if you're one of them, I'm happy for you. I also think you're a liar or a sociopath.

Got it? Are you there, swinging slowly back and forth in that dull malaise? Okay, there you are.

Yes. Now picture a band you've basically never heard of, a band that also happens to be the best rock band of all time, walking out onto a poorly lit stage to a smattering of golf claps and a few ambiguous *woo*s.

You've been waiting for the show to begin with a few friends and a couple of other kids in the humiliatingly named Kiddie Corral section of the club. You're excited to see X, another great band and the reason you're here. The Replacements are a band you've kind of heard of, but you can't remember ever being very impressed with supporting acts. Maybe you're a little bit relieved that the opening act isn't Fools Face again. The parachute-panted and rattailed "New Wave" band that seemed to have some deal with the club that gave them first dibs on being added to the bill any time a band that could even remotely be described as punk/New Wave would roll through St. Louis. All I really remember about them is that they had a lot of belts—red belts, white belts, and black belts, none of which appeared to be functioning with any beltlike usefulness. Oh, and they had synthesizers on those hideous A-frame racks (a half measure for guys who wanted to look cool standing up playing a keyboard but weren't ready to fully commit to the keytar), which was a real deal-breaker for me and most of my friends at the time. They'd play and dance their hearts out in front of an audience that had paid to see someone like Hüsker Dü, just to get booed and have whole cups of beer thrown at them. I didn't like them, but it always made me a bit sad and I could never really figure out why they wanted those slots. So I thought maybe they'd reached the limit of the abuse they were willing to subject themselves to and had finally decided to sit this show out.

So out come the Replacements, looking like they're all wearing some combination of clothes from a specialty shop for tall toddlers and hand-me-downs from the Clash. Fucked-up hair, spray-painted guitars, effortlessly cool in a way I'd never seen before. Fashion without even a hint of trying . . .

"I NEED A GODDAMN JOB, I NEED A GOD-DAMN JOB, I REALLY NEED A GODDAMN JOB, I NEED A GODDAMN JOB!"

And then the chorus . . .

"GODDAMNIT, GODDAMNIT, GODDAMN! I NEED A GODDAMN JOB!"

By now Paul Westerberg had already leaned so far into his microphone that he'd fallen face-first off of the front of the stage onto the empty dance floor. Where he remained for the rest of the song, singing and playing guitar uninterrupted, in various positions: Prone, balancing on his forehead with his mouth pressed against the mic. On his back, craning his neck sideways, 100 percent commitment to the bit.

Except it wasn't a bit. It was as real as anything I'd ever seen. The self-liberating promise of rock 'n' roll, punk rock, whatever you want to call it, come to life, directly in front of my very eyes! I knew I hadn't really witnessed the birth of rock 'n' roll. But I also knew it didn't matter. Because it had been invented inside me that day. This was as close as I'd ever get. I knew what it was. I'd read about it. I'd heard it and believed in it. Like I'm sure people must have read about the lightbulb and marveled at the thought before they ever got to stand in a once-dark room illuminated by electricity. My world shone bright in front of me. I embraced it. I didn't understand it. And I still don't. But it lighted my way.

It wasn't "I need a job and I can't find one." It was "The only thing worse than needing a job is having one." Everything that we're all expected to do and trust and believe in is a total fucking drag. It said to me this above all else: Job or not, I am free—school or not, I am free—as long as this exists—this feeling—this moment where nothing else in the world matters—I will survive—this is where I will choose to live. This is where you will find me.

RAMBLIN' MAN

GATHER 'ROUND, KIDS, AND LET ME TELL YOU THE story of White Pride. Like everywhere else in the 1980s, the St. Louis metropolitan area had a hardcore punk rock scene. Not a big one, but big enough for the punk rock zine *Maximum Rocknroll* to check in every now and then.

White Pride, one of the more notorious bands around town, was a tight little outfit made up of a Jew (lead vox), a half-Chinese guy (who played guitar in full Nazi uniform), another guy who appeared to be of some vague and decidedly non-Aryan ancestry (bass), and a terrifying juvenile delinquent who played a snakeskin drum kit and could spit farther than anyone I've ever seen—continuously launching loogies from behind his kit, back and forth like a lawn sprinkler, over his bandmates' heads and into the pit, for the entire show. Given their mixed pedigree and the fact that Jim, their lead vocalist, looked like a filthy hippie (picture Jim from *Taxi* but with the disposition of a taller, angrier Manson and you're close), their whole shtick came across as pretty solid satire. In reality, the band was made up of mostly older musicians, guys who could really play, who couldn't resist poking some fun at the knuckleheads sporting swastikas and whatnot.

So they named themselves White Pride, threw together some hardcore punk rock songs with unspeakable lyrics, and booked some gigs opening for big-deal national punk bands like Circle Jerks. It was a perfect plan except for one teensy tiny flaw. They were so terrifyingly good at punk rock, and the audiences they played for were so terrifyingly dumb, most people didn't get the joke. I got it. I got that it was a joke. But that didn't make it a good joke or less scary. Still, it's hard to fault them for not stating it explicitly, and I understand that to them clarification would have taken the sting out of the satire. Plus, I'm sure they were thinking the Chinese guy would do the trick and they would never have to explain themselves.

Eventually, they did pull the plug on the whole thing, but not before it all got seriously out of hand. To this day their demos and lone seven-inch single go for big bucks among neo-Nazi collector creeps. Years later, after they shut the band down, I got to be friends with most of them. A couple of the guys got into buying and selling vintage guitars. Bob (the partially Chinese rockabilly Nazi, as we called him, with an interest in expediency and accuracy—there were always lots of Bobs) even toured with Uncle Tupelo briefly as our guitar tech. Their drummer went on to form the legendary Drunks with Guns and eventually join local punk juggernaut Ultraman.

And the guy I was most afraid of, Jim, put together a band called Rugburn with his brother and some other kick-ass musician weirdos. They wore matching pastel polyester tuxes and they'd open up their show with the song "Sunshine on My Shoulders" by John Denver. Except they would change the words to "Rugburn on my shoulders makes me happy, Rugburn on my forehead makes me cry," and "Rugburn almost always makes me HI . . . We're Rugburn!"

Jim and a few of the other guys in the band lived in (or squatted in, I honestly don't know, nor does it matter to our little tale here) an abandoned carpet warehouse they referred to as the "Rugbarn." It was a giant wide-open space, every inch of which was covered in carpet. Not like a single, lovely wall-to-wall short pile. They had taken all of the mismatched carpet remnants left behind by the previous owner and installed them piecemeal onto every available surface in the building. Even the ceiling was carpeted. I know all of this because one night, for some forgotten reason (pity, probably), someone in Rugburn invited me and a few friends over to a party they were throwing after one of their shows.

We were stunned. In our eyes, these were our elders. Rugburn and their friends represented the coolest of the cool to us. Men and women wielding unthinkable power over every living thing in our tiny little scene. You know, local luminaries. We were terrified walking in. It was dark. The party was already in full swing. And by "in full swing" I mean that there were people lounging around on giant rolls of industrial flooring drinking beer with some Coltrane playing softly in the distance. But it occurred to us that the calm could still be a ruse. Like I said, it was dark. Maybe our eyes hadn't adjusted yet and something super scary and satanic was happening in some corner of the room yet to come into focus.

We stood still. Unacknowledged. And just as our sense of danger was fading . . . Jim. The tall, scary singer from White Pride. The one I've had nightmares about. That dude. Jim. Stands up in the middle of the room wearing a fucking banjo and launches into an incredible bluegrass version of "Ramblin' Man" by the Allman Brothers. People are hooting and clapping along. Jim's face is full of sincerity and joy. Just delightful.

I learned something very important that night. Up until that point I had accepted the false premise that punk rock, and art in general, required a coherent philosophy to sustain itself. That lines in the sand must be drawn. Gates must be kept. To make revolutionary art (whatever that is) the past must be razed. Slashed and burned and salted. With one deftly strummed banjo adaptation of a southern rock classic I was relieved of that nonsense. Life's too short to postpone that kind of joy. And for what? "Punk" was never the same.

BLUE NOTE

SOMEWHERE IN THE LATE EIGHTIES, BEFORE WE HAD
any records out, Uncle Tupelo got a call out of the blue
offering us the opening slot for Warren Zevon. At the
Blue Note. In Columbia, Missouri.

That night!

Driving the three hours or so from Belleville to the
Blue Note to see our favorite bands was common prac-
tice in those days. Black Flag, Pixies, Tex and the
Horseheads . . . just to name a few.

So, being offered a show on that stage was pretty
much the pinnacle of our aspirations at the time.

Saying yes. Or, "Fuck yeah!" rather. Loading up and
heading on our way within an hour of the call.

Loading our gear in as Warren Zevon was finishing
his sound check.

Being informed that none of Warren Zevon's stage
setup would be moved to make space for our gear. In-

cluding the grand piano center stage. We were told to figure out how to set up our amps and drums around their equipment.

We were also informed that for our set we would be allowed to use a whopping two channels on the mixing board. Two! So basically we had two vocal mics, and nothing else would be reinforced through the PA.

Looking at the rest of the stage, where Warren Zevon's band was set up. There were microphones literally everywhere. The drum kit had no less than ten. I swear they even had their guitar stands mic'd.

Scanning the stage for any reasonable amount of space for my bass amp. I noticed Timothy B. Schmit from the fucking Eagles making a few last-minute tweaks to his bass sound. Turning knobs on a bass rig that I could hear, clearly, being fed through the front-of-house speakers. A shiny, new, very expensive bass amp in exactly the spot I would have most liked to put my piece-of-shit Peavey bass amp. (The amp I had spray-painted "Pickle River" on for some reason.)

"Hey," I thought, "since only one bass player can play at one time and since Timothy B. Schmit already has a nice sound happening in exactly the place I would love to be able to stand during our set . . . well, maybe he'll be a dear and let me just plug my bass into his rig?"

"Excuse me, Mr. Timothy B. Schmit? Ummm . . . yeah, you guys sound great. Say, I was just wondering, since they're only giving us two mics and we drove all

this way, and on account of me not really having anywhere to put my stuff . . . would it be okay with you if I
just plugged into your shit? I'd totally put the knobs
back the way you have them now. I'm really good about
that . . ."

Timothy B. Schmit holding up one finger signaling
me to stop talking. Angrily, to his bass tech, "DO
NOT LET HIM"—me—"TOUCH FUCKING ANY-
THING."

Almost thirty years later, I sat with Mavis Staples in
the Obamas' box at the Kennedy Center Honors, next
to the Eagles' box. Timothy B. Schmit sat mere feet
away from me.

I don't think he recognized me.

I didn't bring it up.

I wanted to.

But it was Mavis's night.

I think I was reminded of this story by the many
Zevon cover requests I've received over the years. And
maybe as a way to explain why they've all gone unful-
filled. I never really gave him much of a chance after that
night. I hated that whole scene. It's obviously my personal issue. I understand the connection many people
have to Zevon's records. I would never want to diminish
that for anyone.

When I think about this story, I cringe at all the
times in my life where my perceived status and behavior
toward people needing some grace and acknowledgment

from me might have put someone off of my music forever. But the experience at the Blue Note, at that age, was hurtful to me. Of course, now, with hindsight, I understand the ridiculousness and presumptuousness of my request to use the poor guy's precious, personalized bass amplifier. But geez, a simple "Sorry, pal" would've been nice.

HISTORY LESSON- PART II

"OUR BAND COULD BE YOUR LIFE." I GET EMOTIONAL just typing those words. I might not have formulated that exact sentence in my mind back in 1984, but what it said to me was exactly what I most dreamed someone would say to me when I first heard these words.

This song looms so large in my own personal origin story I almost overlooked writing about it. I've been craning my neck looking up to the heavens picking stars out of the sky—songs that have illuminated my path and elevated my hopes. But this song is the ground on which I stand. There is no other song that comes any-where close to defining who I was, what I wished to be, and hopefully where I will always work, and never lose sight of.

During interviews I've given as the band I've been in has endured, and grown, over the better part of three decades, I've frequently been asked, "What are your goals?" And the answer I've most often given to this boilerplate journalistic inquiry has been to claim my highest goal is "getting to keep doing what I do." More recently I've been adding the semi-defeated-sounding phrase "I outlived my dreams a long time ago"—not to sound dramatic but because it's true.

"History Lesson—Part II" was that dream put into not just words but a lived and shared practice and example. The Minutemen was what we (Uncle Tupelo) wanted to be. Sonically, we were informed by them; lyrically, we were emboldened by them; but beyond all of the artistic influence, what we most wanted—what we most saw in them—was a genuine strategy for living that felt both accessible and exalted. More than any of their peers, they spoke to us clearly: Start your own band. Get in the van. What are you waiting for? It was an easy ethos to embrace. It was altruistic and human scaled. Be honest! Make some noise with your friends. Spread the word.

So, for me, once we got past the point where we had a record and a van and gigs to play, I had "made it." Everything that has happened beyond that—bigger stages, record sales, Grammys?!—I've looked at as a challenge to live up to but never as something worthy of a belief system to adhere to. Each treacherous step up the proverbial ladder of success has been taken knowing the comforting fact that nothing has ever made me as happy as having a show to play and a way to get to it.

I ask myself all the time, "Would I still want to tour,

make records, write songs, if the whole scope of my currently pretty cushy lifestyle had to be scaled back to the basics?" "Hell yes!" is the enthusiastic response my heart and brain always give me. And I know it's true, because I have a family of friends and acquaintances equally committed to the simple dream laid out in this one song. Some back in the van after years of buses and stardom, even, and others who never left the van.

In fact, Mike Watt himself has never stopped. Not even after losing D., his best friend, in a catastrophic late-night van accident in the desert a year and a half after this song was released. It was a brutal loss. When he died, in the eighties, it seemed impossible. It felt like a rumor none of us could bring ourselves to believe. In part because of how much life, joy, and sincerity we had just heard him sing in "History Lesson—Part II." "Mr. Narrator, this is Bob Dylan to me . . . but I was E. Bloom and Richard Hell, Joe Strummer and John Doe," and then the heart-stopping last line, "Me and Mike Watt, playin' guitar."

Uncle Tupelo used to play this song in rehearsals and I used to sing the last line as "Me and Jay Farrar, playin' guitar," which used to embarrass Jay a little, I think. And even though we didn't keep that band together, I think it's worth sharing that I still hear that lyric as a testament to Jay's and my friendship and commitment to each other at the time. And I don't think it hurts at all to admit that I may never stand on a stage with him again, but some part of me will always just be "playin' guitar" with Jay. And I doubt there'd be much to share here in this book without this song and a friendship that mirrored its wisdom.

By the way, I bought a T-shirt directly from D. Boon after the Minutemen show Jay and I saw at Mississippi Nights in St. Louis shortly before D. died. He was sweaty and kind and I treasure our brief, wordless interaction. The shirt read "The Roar of the Masses Could Be Farts." Yet another example of how far ahead of their time they were.

LITTLE JOHNNY JEWEL

ONE NIGHT AFTER INGESTING A MISMANAGED AMOUNT of pot cookies, I experienced something I've since learned has a name: ego death. Not only was it not a good time, it was a complete pain in the ass for everyone around me. Which happened to be a van full of my Wilco band-mates and crew. I don't know if you know this, but a packed van isn't a great place to have a meltdown. Also not great—being in a van with someone staring into the abyss. So in hindsight, my heart goes out to all involved.

The evening, when it began, had been beautiful. We were on our way to Wilco's first official show at Liberty Lunch in Austin, Texas, for something called South by Southwest (at the time a showcase festival for newer bands that barely resembled its current incarnation). Everyone was in a good mood. Making good time.

Oklahoma zooming by. Vast expanses of flat prairieland rolling out away from the highway left and right. Half a dozen distant lightning storms dotting the horizon. Spectacular.

Then my brain began to glitch. "Hey, guys, maybe we should grab some food?" I floated the idea knowing it rarely gets rejected. The thought I had was that maybe the beautiful, surreal landscape we were weaving through was too overwhelmingly majestic. I needed to get myself back on terra firma. Find my bearings. Decompress a bit in a comfortable, familiar space. Luckily there was a Taco Bell at the next exit.

Again, things started off lovely. Brightly lit. Everyone ordered their tacos and Taco Supremes and burritos and Burrito Supremes. Staff was unusually chipper. Lots of laughing. In fact, I remember thinking to myself, "This is the most fun I've ever had." And I think it might have truly been. Right up until the moment the face of the Taco Bell employee looking at me from behind the register spun around like a roulette wheel and landed on Beelzebub. Everything seemed to change in an instant. But this time it didn't feel like a passing wave of existential dread. This felt like something had truly broken inside of me. It felt permanent. Between this moment and getting back in the van, my memory gets blurry. I see brief images, like I'm watching a TED Talk PowerPoint presentation on the worst moments of my life—"Here you are vomiting and sobbing, and here we see you re-wrapping your burrito for later, since you were psychotic, not stupid."

Once everyone got me calmed down enough to get back in the van, the consensus was to let me pick the music for a while. One of my favorites at the time (and now) was *The Blow Up*, the band Television's live cassette-only release on the ROIR label, recorded in 1978. I highly recommend it (along with practically the entire ROIR label catalog, by the way), but not as a source of soothing for a broken mind.

Some of the songs are long, but to me that day, they became endless. In fact, I had convinced myself that I was going to die if we ever turned the cassette off or let it stop playing. Over and over again it played through the night, all the way into Texas. Until, I guess, I fell asleep and everyone else in the van gave a quiet cheer, I assume.

I woke up at a truck stop in a little better shape. Still a bit scared and scarred. But functioning. I put on a pair of orange-tinted sunglasses that made everything look happier somehow, so I bought them. There are a few pictures out there of me wearing them, but they're mostly in black and white, so it's hard to tell how ridiculously orange they were.

Years later when I met Richard Lloyd from Television, I told him all about this episode and how "Little Johnny Jewel" simultaneously ripped me apart and held me together. He said, "That's nothing! I once spent a month convinced the radiator in my apartment was playing 'Over Under Sideways Down' by the Yardbirds!" And we laughed. And then we sighed. Both reminded we were lucky to be alive.

SCOTTISH ALARM

BEING AWAKENED BY AN INCREDIBLY LOUD FIRE ALARM mere minutes after dozing off in a large Scottish hotel.

Day three of a UK tour. Day three typically being the hardest day of jet lag effects for this traveler. So very, very tired.

Traipsing down carpeted hallways and staircases and vaguely registering an old building's musty odor mixed with what I can only describe as unfamiliar and un-American-smelling cleaning solutions.

Finding my bandmates and crewmates milling among the other guests in the "car park."

Too tired to talk.

Becoming slightly worried about, and a bit envious of, the members of our entourage who had apparently been able to sleep through the Scottish alarm's incessant nagging metallic pulse.

All clear, we're told. Go back to your rooms. Only a test. At two A.M.! A test.

Long line at the lone refrigerator-sized elevator taking two or three people (max) at a time back to their floors.

Giving up and climbing the four flights back to my room.

Alarm still going. Painfully loud.

Trying to sleep. So tired. Trying to ignore the seemingly broken alarm. Thinking maybe this is my life now. Squeezing my eyes shut. Holding pillows over my ears.

Something whispers in my ear: "Surrender."

I sit up on the edge of the bed and focus my attention on the sound, assuming it's the only thing there is to surrender to. Instead of struggling to NOT hear what is so inescapably there, I start to listen with intention.

What was once brutal, piercing, and painful slowly begins to reveal layers of tones and overtones. The chaos and noise reorders itself into something mesmerizing, beautiful, and complex.

I turn my head and swirls of harmonic nuance dance off of different surfaces in the room.

I turn my head again and swear I can hear the mirror on the closet adding a shimmering, clear top note.

I stand up and move around the room, and what was once a dull monotonous throbbing beat begins to reveal polyrhythms. I suppose thanks to a combination of the perception-altering duration and the very subtle reflections I'm beginning to grasp.

Now I'm wide-awake. I'm inspired.

I can't believe everything I'm hearing is real. I'm hallucinating grand soaring melodies now.

The hair on my arms begins to stand on end.

And then!

It's over. The alarm has stopped. It's silent.

I immediately feel a sense of mourning. I miss the sound. I begin to cry. I feel abandoned.

I sit back down on the edge of the bed.

Now I'm trying to hang on to the sound. I find myself trying to conjure a lingering ghost. I want to keep it with me always now.

The way one glimpse of a smile can carve a deep, indelible impression of a loved one's face to retrieve with the mind's eye—that's how I wish to be able to hear with my "mind's ear(s)" this transcendent aural gift again.

A gift I guess I gave myself by saying yes and surrendering.

The way one might say yes and surrender to the unimaginable power of the ocean. When the waves are crashing in and the only way to not be violently knocked over is to lie down and become a part of the ocean—part of the wave.

At this point in my life I had already developed a

piqued interest in John Cage, noise art, conceptual music . . . I had always been pretty curious when it comes to people making sounds. But I missed emotion and longed for sentiment in music I considered academic. I could not perceive a soul. Only a consciousness. Which, like I said, was exciting enough at that time in my life, so full of discovery and revelations.

Honestly, though, I didn't get it. Most experimental music was hard to feel any connection to.

Until the Scottish alarm explained it to me relentlessly.

The soul I perceived to be missing? My own.

4'33"

IT'S TEMPTING TO ILLUSTRATE THE POINT OF THIS composition—and perhaps the point of this book—by leaving this page blank. Issue a challenge to stare into the void, to journey within and accept that there is no "nothing." Pay attention! The music is YOU.

But I'm afraid, dear reader, that no matter how mild-mannered you may be, you, in turn, might find yourself tempted to slap me around a little bit should we ever cross paths. I would accept my beating with solemn dignity, knowing it to be just and fair. Anyway, it's too late now. I've already sullied the stillness of a blank page—trodden upon the freshly fallen snow, if you will . . . but what's that? You won't? Okay, never mind.

What I'm trying to say is . . . that blank page would have been a great way to get at what I'm trying to say. And since I'm remembering now that John Cage himself wrote a whole book called *Silence*, I'm not going to hesitate or feel bad about adding my own thoughts here. Because I doubt I would have ever thought about songs quite the way that I do without this bold, often misunderstood, even more often maligned, colossally important artistic gesture. This "song," along with "Cartridge Music" and the other experimental records I stumbled upon in the music library at Southern Illinois University Edwardsville while I wasn't going to my classes, changed my life.

My take on this music might not be the most accurate reading of its intentions academically. Honestly, I'm an inspired amateur. I came to this music like an early rock 'n' roll pioneer—by being dumbstruck with curiosity enough to feel compelled to find more at any cost. Picture me sneaking out of Bible studies class to sit in the bushes outside of a speakeasy, but instead of listening to some sweat-soaked rhythm and blues raunching and rolling across the bayou, I'm listening to a piano bench squeak and some coconuts being cracked open with a hot microphone.

ANCHORAGE

MY VERY FIRST BEST FRIEND GROWING UP WAS A GIRL (a tomboy, I was told) who lived six or seven houses away on the opposite side of the street. Whenever I was given permission to go play at her house, my mother would instruct me to cross the street directly in front of our house on my way there. And coming home, I was to wait until I was again directly in front of our house to cross.

In other words, she only wanted me to cross the street in front of our house. The subtext was clear to me—if I was going to get hit by a car, she wanted to watch. No. That's not fair. I guess it's more that she wanted to hear my cries should a car slam into my tiny body. Which is a totally normal motherly thing to desire.

But there was always a lot of confusing subtext with my mom. She was hit by a car on her ninth birthday—"I got a brand-new pair of pink leather cowboy boots and they had to cut them off of me." So there was that. There

WORLD WITHIN A SONG

was also a lot of ominous hinting around that something wasn't right about the family that lived in the dirty white house directly opposite ours. They had a couple of kids my age, but my mom really discouraged me from making friends with them. She'd say stuff like "You can play in their front yard but don't you ever go in their backyard" and "I don't want you to EVER go in their house."

Subtle. Which was fine. They were destructive little shits and I loved my "girl" friend up the street—I mean my friend who happened to be a girl. And on top of that a tomboy . . . so definitely nothing weird going on. But there was something weird going on. Our peers, and the adults in our lives, were slowly but surely making things weird. The kids made fun of us for hanging out because of the whole "cooties" thing. Which honestly we were aware of, but we had chosen to roll the dice based on how much fun we were having. The adults were harder to read. They were obviously uncomfortable with us being so close and our hesitation to play with members of our own sex, but they never really voiced a reason for their concerns. Now, looking back, I think they were clearly worried that we were both gay. Wild times.

Sadly, over time the societal wedges we were facing worked to break us apart, and even sadder, I think, we eventually bought into the idea that there was something wrong with our being friends, to such a degree that, once apart, we kind of never looked back. We had been subtly coerced into being embarrassed about each other and it overpowered our innocence.

What does this have to do with Michelle Shocked and her song "Anchorage"? Not a lot, really. Or everything, maybe. I know of no other song more efficient at getting my eyes wet than this sweet song. I would guess it would have a perfect batting average if tunes were pitches and tears were singles and doubles. I can't even read the lyrics without choking up. And for the life of me, I could never quite understand why this particular song hits me so hard so consistently. It's a simple premise. Two friends grow apart and reconnect through the mail. The bulk of the lyrics are in the voice of Michelle's long-lost friend, bringing her up to date on the twists and turns her life has taken since they last spoke. Lovely stuff.

I think it's the profound air of forgiveness that gets me—the relief of having "walked across that burning bridge" and instead of being met with judgment and resentment, as feared, finding a warm embrace on the other side. After years and years of knowing this song and the power it has over my emotions and not knowing exactly why . . . after having given up on discovering why . . . I finally got my answer.

After a Wilco show in St. Louis in 2010, my aunt Gail walked up to me at the post-show meet-and-greet with a tall middle-aged woman in tow. "Do you know who this is?" she asked.

I wasn't sure I did at first. And then I saw her. The years melted away, and I was face-to-face with my long-lost, beloved very best girlfriend/friend who happens to be a girl. There she was. As we stood beaming at each other, she caught me up on her life. Married. Successful career as an artist. Tenured professor! And as we were winding down—as I was being propelled to the next group of meet-and-greeters—she pulled me in for a hug and said this in my ear: "I've paid attention. I'm so proud of you, my dear, dear courageous friend."

It might be the only time anyone has ever called me courageous to my face. But coming from someone who had only ever seen me as an ultra-sensitive little boy—a boy/friend who happened to be a boy—I accepted the appraisal as a succinct and deeply sincere way of telling me that she knows that, in spite of the outward appearance of having "made it," IT hasn't been easy. A statement of profound empathy. With just a handful of words, she had eased a pain she had witnessed from afar.

I felt whole again knowing we were good. Knowing that we never really stopped being friends—our affection for each other was well chosen and true. And that no one could ever take that away from us.

RENO, NEVADA

DRIVING INTO NEVADA FOR THE FIRST TIME EVER. Twenty extra dollars is agreed upon as a supplement to our per diem for our first foray into legal gambling. Topping a hill on a dark highway, bright lights on the horizon. Reno! We stop, gamble, lose.

Back in the van in under twenty minutes. Pass sign on highway—"Reno 8 miles." A $120 rapid injection into the Sparks, Nevada, economy.

(SITTIN' ON)
THE DOCK OF THE BAY

ARE THERE TOUGHER-SOUNDING OTIS REDDING SONGS?
For sure. Would I play this song for someone to bolster a
claim that he might have been the best soul singer of all
time? No. I would probably play you a live version of
"Try a Little Tenderness." But is this the single most immediately welcoming recording I've ever heard? Yes, I
believe it is.

I'm not sure I can even explain what this song does
to me or put into words how fundamentally this song
shaped my own perception of where one should aim
when writing a song. How high the bar is. It's a perfect
song. Effortless in its execution. Music that understands
itself completely. Betrays no need or desire to impress
beyond its own immaculately drawn conclusions. Saying clearly: Here are the waves. Listen. This is where we
will be for the next 2:47. Can you stop with all of your
overthinking for even just a moment?

It's like getting to hear a song write itself. The music feels like it's conjuring the words being sung. To me, this is the most magical type of song. Even coming out of a cheap AM radio car speaker, this song has the ability to wrap its own world around the listener. It creates a reality and gently surrounds you with it. Your ears see it. The listener is allowed in. To hear it is to be inside it. I am this song. You are this song. We all are.

And what a gift it is to have a song that can transport us somewhere else—take us away from our troubles, allow us a moment free of care . . . what more can a song do? This is the song that taught me all of that—whispered in my ear what I should aspire to. And when you hear the occasional whistled refrain in my own songs, I think I should let you know it's only there because Otis let me sit down on the dock beside him long enough to remember this: Thinking a lot can't really fix a whole hell of a lot. Sometimes, maybe you're better off whistling along with the waves for a while.

YOU ARE MY SUNSHINE

I'VE TRAVELED A LOT IN MY LIFE. ONE OF MY FAVOR-
ite things to do when I'm given the opportunity to live a
day of my life in a city far from my home is walk around.
Sometimes I get to retrace my steps in places I've visited
time and time again. The routine of being in a touring
rock band has allowed me to get to know most of the
major cities on a few continents by now. Occasionally,
we go somewhere we haven't been, and I get even more
excited to explore the new city on foot.

But I'm pretty content, in general, just getting to
traipse around almost anywhere I find myself. I end up
well acquainted with cool buildings, well-planned city
centers, shaded river walks, great local restaurants . . .
sometimes I'll even find myself taking a path I've taken
before, just to revisit a particular tree in a park in Am-
sterdam, or a memorial beside a bike path in Portland,
Maine, for some kids who died in a car crash.

I don't really think about it much. It just kind of happens. Like, "Oh, here's that leaning cemetery wall," or "I know where I am! If I keep walking in this direction there'll be a Victorian-era greenhouse on the left." I think this habit derived from an impulse to remind myself of where I've been. It's oddly comforting to think of something I've seen before and find out it still exists. Or see if it's changed or how much it's changed . . . and when I make the effort to check my memory of the past against the reality of my present, I often find myself staring at a rusty old bike lock I made a mental note of for some reason, and my brain will say something like, "Well, look at us, we're both still here, how 'bout that . . . you and me, you rusty old heart-shaped bike lock engraved with 'W.G. + F.S. Forever' hanging off of a fence on a bridge over the Rhine in Cologne. Good job, everyone!"

And then I head back to the hotel. One thing I discovered after many years of falling in love with weird specific bike locks, park trees, and "in memory of" stone benches around the world is that this attention to detail and piqued curiosity about my surroundings tends to dull considerably when I get home. I don't spend a lot of time walking around Chicago with the same sense of geological time spinning my mind toward the poetry of place. I enjoy getting out in the neighborhood and moving my body, but everything tends to blur a bit compared to my visits to less-familiar environs.

But occasionally I have these moments where it all hits me—the filter of familiarity that colors everything mundane falls from my eyes, and it's glorious again. I can see it all anew with the eyes that accompany me on my travels. I'll ask myself, "How is it possible to take all of this beauty for granted?" And when this happens, I always think of "You Are My Sunshine," and how there hasn't been a single moment of my life where this song felt unknown to me. I think about how long it took before I even thought of it as a song. And even longer before I contemplated the fact that someone had to have written it. An individual human person had made it up before anyone else had ever heard it.

How is it that this song can feel like it has always existed? Weren't we all just born to this song? Born to breathe this song like the air in our lungs? It's easy to overlook the blue in the sky, I guess. But it's important to come home and be reminded of how special it is. How does a song become a home? The same way houses do. People have to live in them. Life has to happen inside of them. Laughing, crying, shouting. A song is a home when it matters not at all who's singing it, young or old. It's built for any voice.

I work to never forget that it's also the greatest song ever written. There's no place like home.

RAUNCH HANDS

TRYING TO BOOK A BAND I LIKED CALLED THE RAUNCH Hands in the mideighties. Having no idea what I was doing, but calling the number on their record and hoping for the best. Reading the contract and equipment rider they sent me. Standard requests—money, a certain-size PA, cases of beer, pizza . . . stuff like that.

Whistling to myself in that distinct soft, descending way that says, "Um . . . not good." Realizing I had no idea what I was doing. Knowing they'd eventually figure out that I had no idea what I was doing. Which, judging by the lack of follow-up, happened fairly quickly.

I WILL ALWAYS
LOVE YOU

BUCKLE UP. BECAUSE WHAT I'M ABOUT TO SAY IS GO-ing to provide some solid evidence to support the inarguable wisdom behind my never having the log-in information for my own social media accounts. In fact, for years now, I've adhered to a strict fail-safe protocol. One that requires two keys to be entered and turned at the same time before firing off a tweet or gram or tik and/or tok.

At least that's how my "team" explains the process. To be sure, at this very moment I'm sweating a bit. I'm beginning to rethink the judiciousness of sharing what I'm about to share. This opinion is controversial in what was once a low-stakes kind of way. Decidedly. But there's really no such thing as low-stakes in this era where simply "liking" someone else's post, absentmindedly, could lower your stock. It's an outrage economy and I don't want anything to do with it. Still, ill-advised as it may be, I think my long-held assessment of this song is worth talking about to serve a broader point.

I don't like this song. I think it stinks. Doesn't matter who sings it. It fries my nerves. If I had to single out one main offense, it'd be the AAAAAAAYYYYYY-EEEE-EYE part. I hate that. I think I have a tough time with extra syllables being added to long notes in general. Maybe because, as a singer, I'm not very good at it. That's definitely something I've learned over the years. People tend to diminish or dismiss stuff they're bad at. Musicians are hilariously consistent with this quirk. Now, when I'm talking shop with someone in a band (let's call him Johnny) and he says something absurd, like "No harmony vocal has ever improved a rock recording," I think to myself, "Johnny must suck at singing harmonies." So it's not like I don't get that I'm the problem here. I would never argue with someone about it. I'm sincerely happy for you if you're into it.

And it's not like I haven't tried. I have. Trust me, I've tried to like this song. Because other people love it, for one thing. And because I adore Dolly Parton. So, tell us, Jeff, why share such a negative view? Thank you, I'm glad you asked. Because I think it's okay to admit everything isn't made for you. Or that nothing is made for everyone. It's okay to not "get" something. I think it's important to feel free to dislike something other people lose their minds over. And because this is a book, and I'm not opening up the floor for debate. If this somehow irritates someone to the point they're compelled to "come at me" online, I won't care. I mean, I'm not going to see it. And even if I did, I wouldn't care enough to request the launch codes to respond.

So I might as well share this part, too . . .

One of the things people always marvel at about Dolly is that she wrote this song and "Jolene" in the same day. When I heard that for the first time, I thought to myself, "That's pretty impressive, but at least one of those two songs sucked." I possibly thought that so I could go back to feeling okay with myself as a hardworking songwriter.

So, just to be clear, I LOVE Dolly Parton! She's the best. Person, songwriter, singer. You name it, she's the best. All I'm saying is that "Jolene" was enough work for one day. Geez . . . why are you looking at me like that?

WANTED DEAD OR ALIVE

BON JOVI POSSESSES THE TYPE OF ARROGANCE THAT compels one to swing for the fences every time one steps to the plate (microphone). Every song is angling to be a world-changing anthem. It's completely alien to me.

So I reflexively reject everything Bon Jovi does. In fact, I hate it so much I'd like to retract my previous words advocating for allowing space for everyone to like what they like and despise what they despise. I was wrong. This song sucks and you should not like it. I guess I hadn't really contemplated this song thoroughly enough before I got all altruistic back there in that "I Will Always Love You" chapter.

SPIN SHOOT

DOING A COVER SHOOT FOR *SPIN* MAGAZINE IN THE late aughts with a bunch of other artists. It was their summer festival issue and the premise was that we were all in line for a porta-potty.

It became clear after a while that they were probably going to try for a foldout cover, because there were too many people to fit on the front page.

Publicists and managers were swooping in and demanding better placement for their artists. Everyone wanted to be in the back of the line because the porta-potty was going to be the punchline reveal when the cover was folded out.

I don't even remember how I ended up where I did.

But I did meet RZA!

"Your shoe's untied," he said, pointing down at my dirty white low-top Converse tennis shoes.

"Um . . . yeah, I know, thanks," I said.

"That your thing?" he queried.

"Yeah, kinda," I said. Truth being, I'd given up on trying to keep them tied.

"Cool." He nodded, adding, "That used to be my thing."

I love that guy. Might be the coolest I've ever felt.

BEFORE TONIGHT

THIS SONG BY THE BAND SOULED AMERICAN IS LIKELY the hardest track to find of any I've included here in this weird little book of love letters to songs. These guys were from Illinois. A little bit older band than Uncle Tupelo, but we traveled in the same "circuit," for lack of a word more accurate to describe the hodgepodge of Midwestern bars, clubs, and college cafeterias our tours were all comprised of.

I'd like to say I saw them play a lot, but owing to their habit of playing in near-total darkness, I'm not sure I ever really "saw" them at all. I definitely would have had trouble picking them out of a lineup. Matching each instrument and its player was certainly out of the question.

My wife, Susie, knew them all pretty well. The carved wooden animals that adorned the façade of her former club, Lounge Ax, were made by Jamey Barnard, who played drums in the band up until 1991. Jamey was also an insanely talented comic—possibly the best phone prankster of all time. His genius twist on the form being his ability to get people to call HIM. He'd lay traps by filling out the forms one used to find at checkout counters advertising too-good-to-be-true credit card deals and time-shares. (Again, it might be worth reminding people how most of the grifts and cons we associate with the internet predate the digital age and possibly even the printing press.)

Unwitting salespeople working in the dark ages of telemarketing would nonchalantly place the noose around their own necks by calling Jamey to discuss his possible interest in a cemetery plot, for example, and he'd record them reacting to absurd situations and characters he'd improvise on the spot. "I'm sorry if I sound frazzled, I'm just not sure what I'm going to do about all of this blood," or "I'd love to come by and talk in person . . . would you mind meeting at dawn?" Genius.

It's possible that the cassette recordings of the prank calls that Jamey gave Susie all those years back are easier to find online than some of Souled American's music. Worth looking for. We cherish our cassettes to the point of having had them backed up digitally more than once out of fear the tape will degrade beyond playability.

But this song doesn't have a whole lot to do with Jamey or prank calls. What I think first and foremost when I hear this song is the same thing I thought the first time I heard it—"I wish I could have written this."

It's the perfect combination of the metaphysical and the mundane—the cosmic and the commonplace. In general, it's about time. And how time moves at maddeningly inconsistent speeds dependent upon our moods and states of mind.

Even the way the song is performed contributes to the poetry. I'm always a sucker for a band all pointed in the same direction yet unconcerned with metronomic time. Like a group of friends walking toward the next bar—sometimes together, at other times in pairs, maybe someone is running to catch up after stopping to take a leak behind a dumpster, and then all together again. It's a beautiful feat to stretch musical time like that. Maybe a little undervalued in western music. It takes a lot of trust in each other as a band to allow a song to just happen as opposed to being performed.

It's an intimate act to agree upon, not being perfect. I'm moved by it every time. And as a set of lyrics, it's hard for me to resist quoting the entire song. But I'll restrain myself and just share this, which is what lies at its heart. And has been on my mind for decades now . . .

A song before a voice
A chance before a choice
A lamp before a light

Stuck with today
Before tonight
A spool before a wind
A found after a find
A youth before a past
At least before . . .
At last

SHOTGUN

WHEN MY WIFE, SUSIE, AND I WERE MARRIED, ON A miserably hot August evening in 1995, she was unmistakably pregnant, with five and a half months' worth of baby Spencer growing inside of her body. The ceremony was held in Chicago at the rock club she co-owned with her partner, Julia, on Lincoln Avenue, across from the Biograph Theater and the alley next to it where John Dillinger was killed after being ratted out by another moviegoer or his date, "the lady in red," depending on whom you ask.

But that night, *Nine Months* was the movie being advertised on the theater's marquee. It was a fun wedding. Some family attended. My dad brought his own cooler of beer from downstate, even though we had assured him we had him covered, Lounge Ax being a bar and all. But most of our guests were our friends from the local music community we loved so much and felt so connected to. And they loved us enough to surprise us with a ragtag marching band to march us down the "aisle." If you were in a band in Chicago in the midnineties and had a horn or a snare drum lying around, there's a good chance you were at our wedding. Thank you.

Our friend Lana, an extraordinarily gifted cocktail waitress ordained by the Universal Life Church, officiated. Susie and I stood on the stage, said our vows, and stepped on a glass (tradition!). And when the kick-ass rhythm and soul band we had hired for the party joined in, they played the only truly obvious song we could have requested if we'd thought about it: "Shotgun," by Junior Walker and the All Stars.

Now, don't get me wrong—there are a lot of ways the idea of a "shotgun wedding" is uncool. And if we were more uptight, we might have felt the need to set the record straight. Truth is, I wasn't being coerced to "make it official" and marry Susie. In fact, I felt like I was lucky she wanted to marry me at all. If you knew me at the time, it would have been hard to imagine what she thought she was getting in the bargain. But on the other hand, it was a funny song to play, and everyone got a big kick out of it. She was pregnant, after all.

So this song comes up a lot in our house. When we get to talking with new friends or neighbors about how we got together, I always hear this in my head . . .

Shotgun!
Shoot him 'fore he run now

ROCK CLUB GHOST SHIP

EARLY NINETIES. ARRIVING FOR SOUND CHECK IN Houston at an unlocked venue only to find it completely vacant and with the eerie sense that all humans, staff and clientele alike, who were once here have now vanished. Cigarettes smoldering, blurry melting iced cocktails sweating on the bar—like some kind of underground rock club ghost ship.

Following the unmistakable hollow gurgling sound of a massive bong hit, leading us to the corner perch of what appears to be the venue's lone survivor—the house sound man.

Being mesmerized by the absolutely Cheech-ian (or possibly Chong-ian) cloud of smoke emanating from and blotting out the face of the house "sound dude" as he informs us that the PA we are currently supposed to be sound checking with has been lent to a friend and will "probably" be back around midnight. He suggests we go "chill out at Denny's" and come back at midnight. The xeroxed flyers in the entryway say "Uncle Tupelo 10 P.M."

Starting our set at two A.M. Five attendees. No paying customers. Just the band that brought the PA back and the sound dude.

THE WEIGHT

EVERYBODY KNOWS AND LOVES THIS SONG. OR AT least every musician I've ever met. Although I'm ashamed to admit I once moderated my high opinion of the Band, and this song in particular, because of a Robert Crumb interview where he used "The Weight" as an example of how ridiculous and corny his musical contemporaries were. He could have just said he strongly preferred Dixieland jazz and early string band 78s, but he's entitled to his opinion.

The shameful part is how it stuck in my head for so long. And because I liked his art and shared with him an affinity for early recordings and the unparalleled excitement of getting to hear new forms in their infancy, I had a period where I kind of agreed with him. Looking at the Band's album jackets, I'd think to myself, "Look at these carpetbagging Canucks posing like they just robbed the Southern Pacific mail train, with their bushy beards and waistcoats . . . pfff!"

Now, some of you who've been following my career might be thinking, "Um, excuse me, Jeff, but I seem to recall you spending a good portion of your public life standing underneath hats and singing through a beard." I hear you. It's a weird disconnect. But it doesn't need to make sense. Because it's true. I have often donned and appropriated the styles of those whose authenticity I found suspect. I'm sure if I had the energy for such a topic I could rationalize my sartorial choices as being an extension of my desire to simultaneously embrace and subvert traditional American folk music forms. But in doing so I would sound like an asshole. So let's just agree that it's hard to find stuff to wear onstage. Especially when you aren't particularly interested in the showbiz side of things. So somebody gives you a hat and you put it on, and someone else, maybe a publicist or someone in your band, tells you that you "look good" and says, "Man, you should rock that onstage." And before you know it, you're standing at a microphone years later looking out at an audience full of guys wearing "your" hat.

Let's get back to "The Weight," shall we?

Eventually I realized R. Crumb was kind of a creep for being so closed-minded about rock music, and maybe even kind of a creep in general. So I was able to reclaim both the Band and "The Weight" with unabashed fervor.

Of course, the other element that I've failed to

mention—the one performance most responsible for making the song unassailable to myself and almost every musician I've ever met—is the movie *The Last Waltz*'s rendition with the Staple Singers. As great as the original studio recording of this song is, it doesn't have Mavis Staples. I've watched it a thousand times and I still can't understand the full ramifications of what it tells us about Mavis's singular talent. Pure commitment, entirely free of pretense, a range of emotions on display in one line that surpasses what most other singers could summon up in an entire career . . . and above all else, the thing I think it's impossible to find more of in any other footage of any other artist: joy.

With this one sublime performance, Mavis goes beyond just inhabiting a song, as all other musicians strive to do. She inhabits herself—her own skin—so completely, so free of judgment, so visibly generous in her spirit, that to see it is to be changed. It made such an impression on me that when we met years later I had to hide my shock that she wasn't, as I had pictured her, nine feet tall. If humanity at some point in the future is ever put on trial before a galactic body, I hope this footage still exists, because I can think of nothing more redeeming for all of us than to witness Mavis in all her glory.

WILL YOU LOVE ME TOMORROW

LIKE SO MANY OF MY OTHER FAVORITE SONGWRITERS I've been writing about, Carole King could easily have been the sole focus of this book if all I wanted to discuss was songcraft. Picking fifty of her songs would have been a piece of cake. And in terms of sharing what I've learned from other songwriters just by listening to their records, I can't think of anyone more important to me.

But in writing this, I'm trying to get at something beyond the contributions made by the songwriters themselves. I'm much more fascinated by the blurry area between a song and the mind that receives it, puts it back together in a shape that fits their own life, and allows the heart to take ownership. In my case I have the added mystery of how being a singer of other people's songs in front of an audience becomes so deeply personal, and leaves me feeling more exposed than even the most emotionally naked of my own songs.

There was a period in my life, back in the early Wilco days, when singing this song as an encore—a ballad that I would often deliver lying on my back while being held aloft and passed by the outstretched arms of fans, crowd surfing in slow motion—felt like I was being as honest as I could ever be with an audience. Will you still love me tomorrow? All of you. Will you? Because this night is forever to me. I can feel you . . . I sense you mean it right now in this moment . . . I can allow myself to trust you. But you're going to move on, aren't you?

It's a hard thing to admit sometimes as performers, but we need you. And I wouldn't be within a thousand feet of a stage if I didn't desperately want to feel this connection. I want to be seen. I want to feel special. But you're seeing other bands, aren't you?

As ridiculous as that all sounds, it's a true revelation of an internal dialogue that is always happening just below the surface of any song I'm singing. Singing "Will You Love Me Tomorrow" back in the day was my effort to come clean. I'm in love with you people out there listening. Please don't hurt me.

GERMAN BURGER KING

LEAVING A BRIEFCASE CONTAINING OUR ENTIRE TOUR'S net income under a table at a truck stop Burger King in Germany. Discovering this fact an hour after we'd gotten back on the autobahn.

Returning two hours after we had left and finding it in the exact same spot where we left it. Eating again.

FREE BIRD

AS I WRITE THESE WORDS IN 2023, IT FEELS OBVIOUS to me that what I'm about to say should be unnecessary. Alas, dear reader, it remains a scourge that must be addressed. Here goes: Yelling "Free Bird" in any context is dumb. It's not clever or funny. It makes YOU look bad. Since about 1989 everyone who has participated in this little stunt has woken up the next morning ruing the decision to yell "Free Bird." I'm not trying to be mean. Don't do it. Save yourself.

My life onstage has been peppered every step of the way by this inane occurrence. Setting aside the undue burden this has placed on my life, the world "Free Bird" created for itself is exactly what this book is about.

Sometimes, the life a song takes on when unleashed upon a chaotic society can become monstrous. Lynyrd Skynyrd didn't want this. They wrote an ode to restless liberty (and shameless romantic conquest, perhaps). And now look at it . . . it's a punch line to the worst joke on earth. The music side of the song was stripped and sold for parts. The title alone stands. A proto-meme. Hearing it from the stage or audience is as close to Rickrolling as we could get back in the pre–World Wide Web before-times.

Now that Rickrolling itself has passed its sell-by date, I feel like everyone should just know not to request "Free Bird." Sadly, I can feel my words falling on deaf ears. And I fear only draconian measures like immediate re-movals and lifetime venue bans could once and for all set us all free from this vibe-killing menace. We've trav-eled far past the "they know not what they do" plea for leniency. So I'll just have to beg you, please, don't do it.

Do, however, throw on "Free Bird"—the actual song, yes—sometime and marvel at the truly spectacular guitar interplay that comes close to fully erasing the pathetic self-aggrandizing lyrics from the front half, the ballad half of the song. Pee-wee Herman telling Dottie not to fall in love with him because he's "a loner, a rebel" was more convincing. Geez. Now I want to hear it!

THE STAR-SPANGLED BANNER

"NO WAY, THANK YOU, BUT NO." THAT'S WHAT I SAID without hesitation when my next-door neighbor asked me over our backyard fence if I'd ever be interested in singing the national anthem at a sporting event.

He wasn't just asking idly; he happened to be an employee of one of the major sports teams in Chicago. Kind of high up, even. So he was a guy who could make it happen. We were friends. Still are, even though he and his awesome wife and dogs moved out of the city a few years ago. But I still think it hurt his feelings when I elaborated by telling him that I think it's a terrible song. "It's militaristic, and even if I liked it, it's too hard for a guy like me to sing.

"If they ever change the national anthem to something more reasonable, hit me up," I added as he clapped his golden retriever up to his porch to go back inside.

With hindsight, I can see that I handled the question tactlessly.

However, I stand by it. The idea of America—the promise of these United States—deserves better than a crappy battle song. If it were up to me, I think I'd try to sell everyone on the idea of something with a wordless melody everyone can sing. Like the riff from "Seven Nation Army," but I guess that might conjure up the same sort of "Fuck you, world" we were trying to avoid.

I know!

Stevie Wonder is still alive; let's get him to write us a celestial anthem that glows in the dark. Before it's too late.

THE *MARY* F***ING *CELESTE*

WALKING AROUND INSIDE THE WARNER BROS. BUILD-
ing in Burbank, California, with my then manager
looking for someone who could direct us to the head of
A&R's office. Realizing that we strolled right in without
the usual security stop and hadn't seen a single person
since entering. Beginning to notice half-eaten sandwiches
on desks and other odd evidence that people had left in
some type of hurry. Going floor to floor, shouting hello
up and down hallways—nothing. The *Mary* fucking *Ce-
leste*. Giving up and heading toward the exits. Two security guards informing us the building was about to be
declared "all clear" after a bomb threat.

Pre-9/11.

Learning that bomb threats against record label HQs
were fairly common. Common enough that, upon threat
notification, everyone we were supposed to meet had
calmly walked over to the commissary on the WB lot for

lunch. Not one person thought they should try to get ahold of the Wilco guy and give him a heads-up?

Daydreaming about how high on the list of crazy rock-related deaths my demise would have ranked had an actual bombing of the WB building occurred with the only victims being myself and my manager.

Not to mention the conspiracy theories that would form.

I mean, I wasn't even scheduled to perform. Had just flown in that morning for a meeting about my "career." Why was I there? Was it a setup? Where was security?

Meeting a bust.

RADIO FREE EUROPE

WHEN I COME ACROSS EARLY R.E.M. SONGS IN THE wild now—a restaurant playlist, the occasional hip elevator—they hit me the way a vague early childhood sense memory might. Like how a musty smell might take you back to your grandparents' root cellar—no specifics attached, just a bodily reminder that you were also you, alive, in the past and that you inhabited spaces you no longer have access to without the gentle coaxing of a certain type of light or smell.

The crazy thing is, R.E.M. songs started out this way, at least for me. Hearing them for the first time felt like my earlier thoughts and feelings were being recollected. For kids like me and my friends, it was disorienting and intoxicating to have new music that felt somehow old. Songs that radiated sincerity yet gave only a lip of soft clay as a foothold for meaning.

These were our thoughts—our confused internal

dialogues—our wild curiosity, muffled by the slight em-
barrassment of our own earnestness being sung back to
us. At the time it didn't even feel like the band themselves knew what to make of it all. And their bewilder-
ment fed our belief in them. Listening to them was an
act that felt on equal footing with their intent. The general laws of capitalism usurped by a gift economy where
giving was getting and vice versa, but "money" wasn't
part of the equation.

Of course, it was all a bit of a youthful fantasy. Like
everyone else, R.E.M. wanted hits, and wanted to get
paid. And, of course, they deserved to be paid. But that
never stopped me from holding deep and cherishing the
idea that music belongs to both sides, the creator and the
listener. Feeling ownership of music you didn't make
through the simple act of investing yourself into it will
always be more real to me than whatever goes on at the
New York Stock Exchange.

The main difference? You can't put a price on it.

I'M AGAINST IT

AS I GET OLDER, I'M FINDING IT HARDER AND HARDER to comprehend how a miracle like the Ramones happens. How are they real? How is it that something like the Ramones ever occurred outside of someone's imagination? The mystery deepens when you take in the fact that they're all gone. Every original "Ramone" has now shed this mortal coil. If I think about it too much, I start to find the argument for the existence of a higher power more compelling. Maybe there is a GOD!

Oddly enough, the evolutionary theories regarding randomness, genetic mutation, and natural selection also get bolstered by contemplating my favorite band, ever, from Queens. Either explanation—god or spontaneous mutation—feels weak on its own. Together, the normally opposing concepts start to make sense.

The truth is, I should stop thinking so hard. I'll never

understand. I should just say "What the FUCK?!" and move on. You know, "let the mystery be," as Iris De-Ment says in one of my favorite songs ever. What I should focus on is my good fortune. Thank my lucky stars I walked the earth at the same time as these weirdos.

As for the songs themselves, it's hard to pick just one. And in a way, individually, they don't matter. Favorites aside, what matters is the travail—the discipline and gargantuan levels of self-possession required to create not just a "band" with "songs" but to invent a world where every gesture is iconic. Everything from white canvas sneakers and leather jackets to how a song gets counted in onstage is, ostensibly, a fully considered addition to the big picture. All contours clearly defined— and yet, artistic choices seemingly spontaneous and blind, i.e., not "choices" at all. Which also makes plain some unmistakable genius at work—sharp, deliberate, and permanent.

All of this is to say I ADORE the Ramones. If I haven't heard them for a while, tears of joy shoot out of my eyes like windshield wiper fluid when we're re-united.

This song? "I'm Against It"? Well . . . I'm for it. The lesson learned from having this song in my life is pre-cious to me. We CAN have joy and OWN our alien-ation at the same time. These lyrics are funny and dumb, but to me they're as profound as any other proper poetry I've ever met. The way I see it, at some point saying what you hate transcends negativity—it becomes liberating. It's "punk" rock math. A thousand no's adds up to one big fucking YES!

COACHELLA

FIRST FEW DAYS IN REHAB. I WAS A BASKET CASE. STRUG-
gling with full-blown panic attacks all day long. Just
really wiped out, and not thinking about being a musician. And certainly not thinking that anybody who
worked at this hospital knew who I was or had any
interest in what I was doing.

Young guy on the night shift, coming into my room
and asking, "I was just curious, are you guys still playing
Coachella?"

"What do you think?"

"My friends and I are going, I was just curious if you
were still going . . ."

"I'm in the hospital . . ."

We did cancel.

BIZCOCHITO

I WISH I'D TAKEN SPANISH WHEN I WAS IN SCHOOL. Most kids I knew in high school did. A few took German. But I chose French, for some reason that eludes me to this day. Not that it would have mattered. Had I taken Spanish, I'm sure I would have been just as good at not learning that language as any other. Let's just say, cher lecteur, mon français c'est de la merde!

Now, after traveling quite a bit in Europe I can generally grasp enough of what's being spoken around me to grok the gist. But I still get sad that I wasn't able to apply myself to learning at least one other language. And when I first heard Rosalía's music, that agonizing sense that I had missed out on some precious life-enhancing knowledge by neglecting to grow another tongue hit me harder than ever.

However, being on the outside looking in didn't stop me from falling in love with Rosalía's voice and her crazy run of artistic quantum leaps. So I kept listening. And listening. And listening. And before long I started noticing something profound happening. I started to believe I could understand what she was saying most, if not all, of the time. Not literally. Emotionally.

It then shocked me when I started googling English translations of her lyrics and realizing my theory—the possible wishful thinking of a mono-language dope—could hold water. I was more than just in the general ballpark based on half-understood Spanish phrases sneaking through the mix. I wasn't just grabbing on to fragments and putting together a plausible story. I could actually hear the look on her face. I could see the man she was singing to—pinpoint the heartache to a specific moment in her life.

In this song—way before I ever checked out the literal translation—I had perfectly understood the scope of how succinctly she could tell someone who might dare to underestimate her to back the fuck off. Now, I understand what you might be thinking: "That's not that impressive, all songs create meaning outside of directly understood lyrics. Most of us are clearly performing these feats of listening without trying to make ourselves out to be some kind of genius listener."

To which I say, I get it. I agree. But my point isn't that it's just me and my well-honed ears unlocking the "Rosalía stone." I'm saying that, yes, it's typical for musical keys and vocal inflections, etc., to shape what we take away from a song—that's a fact. But I'm also arguing that no one on earth has ever sung that extra layer of nonlanguage meaning as virtuosically and clearly at the same time. The lyrics themselves are snotty, revealing, playful, aggressive, lurid, innocent, funny, morbid, joyous, defiant . . . just full to the brim with life.

But the ability to sing two languages at once, one inside of the other, is where she makes the case for herself as a generational talent. It reminds me of the recent discoveries in how a bird's song is perceived by other birds. Which has revealed that while we're hearing the simple "whippoorwill" of a whippoorwill, for example, another whippoorwill is able to discern massive amounts of microtonal variation imparting different types of information within the same song.

I can't explain it further, but it makes sense to me. It also makes sense to me that Rosalía's first discipline was flamenco (in which she has a master's degree). And while I can't claim to understand all of the implications of why that particular starting point makes perfect sense, I do know that it's a folk tradition that employs what appear to be microscopically calibrated gestures and variances to tell the most dazzling, passionate story one can pull from oneself.

On top of all of this top-tier vocal talent and emotional intelligence, Rosalía is forging a path for herself

artistically in a way that looks positively Dylan-esque to
a Dylan-obsessed fellow like myself. How's that for taking something so clearly belonging to the world at large
and grinding it through the old-white-guy lens? But
there really are parallels. Taking something old and
making it sound modern is nothing new. She's done that.
Dylan did that.

But beyond that, to transform timeworn musical
forms into shapes that sound like a new type of future,
and do so repeatedly and seemingly at will, deserves recognition alongside people like Miles Davis and Picasso.

In fact, I'd be willing to bet that at some point in the
future, those iconoclasts might end up being referred to
as the Rosalías of their time. The major difference, of
course, being that she's an enormous international pop
star already. No critical reevaluation of Rosalía's work
will be necessary for the masses to catch up. She somehow
manages to wrap all of her bold moves and innovations
inside utterly irresistible pop shapes. If she were a painter,
I would say at some point she stopped painting on canvas
and just started replacing everyone's eyes with a new
type of eye. Eyes designed for the invisible colors at the
edges of the rainbow. When Rosalía sings, life looks and
sounds different. Everything is a new, previously unex-
plored possibility.

Admittedly, I could have picked another song to talk
about. Perhaps one that better illustrates the direct lin-

eage to the folk tradition she has emerged from. But this song makes me so goddamn happy I didn't want to pass up a chance to put it in front of someone new. Besides, you should be listening to all of what she has to offer anyway. Come get your new eyes!

THE BEATLES

THIS IS THE ONLY BAND I'M GOING TO WRITE ABOUT without picking a single song. And you know why, don't you? Because it's impossible. On top of the fact that I've formed a deep personal relationship with their entire catalog, they're the only band I can feel 100 percent certain that anyone who might pick up this book has formed some opinion of through their own experience.

Everyone loves the Beatles. Even people who hate the Beatles know they should love them, and what they're reacting to negatively isn't the actual Beatles—it's their ubiquitousness, their largeness. Or maybe one's own feeling of having had them foisted upon them by everyone. If someone tries to tell you that the Beatles were actually bad at music, or that they objectively think they sucked, you're talking to a person without ears or a heart or a mind or possibly even a BODY! You should run from that miserable demon before they make you sick.

All you need to do to understand the universal appeal of the Beatles is find yourself in the same room as a kid (infant on up) hearing them for the first time. It's instantly clear to them—"This is great, where have you been keeping this stuff?!" Like how we managed to not let Spencer have any sugar until we broke down on his first birthday and bought him a cake. I swear, literally one second after a single molecule of chocolate icing reached his tongue, his face changed into a look that we had never seen before. A face I can only describe as possessed . . . but possession by way of some cute version of Satan, or maybe the "Trix are for kids" rabbit. While we sat paralyzed by his expression, he immediately lunged for the cake and hugged it to his chest. You know . . . like the Beatles. You get it. I'm not going to waste any more of your time. Go enjoy your own connection to the Fab Four.

I will say that having the Beatles in the world can feel pretty daunting as a musician. Everyone doing what I do kind of knows the world already has the Beatles. It's incredibly unlikely any of us will get anywhere close to that kind of impact. Culturally, that is. Musically, they're the opposite. They're a shining beacon for everyone to steer toward if you choose to aim your art outward, openly giving and reaching for love. The scale of the magical structure they built is unattainable, but the sandbox is still full of the same sand—we're all allowed to build with the same material. And we've even been encouraged, by them, to think in new shapes.

One of the most pivotal moments in my life as a musician was when the *Beatles Anthology* series was released. At the time, there was little out there to suggest anything other than polished, visionary record-making from the Beatles. They weren't a band that had been bootlegged nearly as much as a lot of other artists. I suspected and craved confirmation that they had to have sounded human (bad, or at least not perfect) at some point in the process of album-making. So when these collections of demos, early takes, rough mixes, and outtakes came out, I felt I'd been handed a treasure map. A schematic of love, clear and readable enough to reverse-engineer any type of tune. Did "Strawberry Fields" always sound like music made by an underwater candy orchestra? Why, no. Here you can listen to it how it was written. Like a normal song strummed on an acoustic guitar. What about "Helter Skelter"? That must have just been lightning striking, right? First take, perhaps? Visionary proto-metal, quantum-leap guitar onslaughts like that must be born of a clear bolt out of the blue. Nope. Just a tepid blues trudge here. Fascinating nonetheless, because YOU know they're onto something, even though they don't quite sound like they'll ever get there.

It's truly hard to overstate how important it was to be given the validation of knowing that even the Beatles struggled, made wrong turns, changed course, and ultimately surrendered to each unsure moment as an invitation to swim in a starlit sky of possibility. I was given permission to sound bad on my way to sounding great by these records. Bad with gusto and an unabashed joyful wonder. No one looks inside and discovers only diamonds and pearls. If art is at least in part an act of discovery, you might as well learn how to enjoy getting lost, too.

ABBEY ROAD

BEING TOLD BY THE TICKET AGENT AT O'HARE THAT my passport had expired mere days before the date on my ticket. Abbey Road mastering session set to begin in eighteen hours.

Going straight from O'Hare to the Federal Building downtown to get in line for an expedited passport renewal. *Yankee Hotel Foxtrot* master tapes in tow.

After six hours downtown, heading back to O'Hare with shiny new expedited miracle passport to catch the overnight flight to London Heathrow.

Taking a black cab directly from Heathrow to Abbey Road. Somehow arriving only an hour late.

Good news—being sort of on time with *YHF* reels intact.

Bad news—cabin pressure on the flight rendered me deaf in my right ear. Miserable and frustrated.

Meeting and informing mastering engineer Steve

Rooke of my monophonic hearing situation. "Steve, I'm afraid I won't be of much value today. I can only hear out of my left ear."

"Well, Jeff, we should be fine, because I can only hear with my right ear. Let's sit side by side and between us we'll have a good pair of ears," Steve said dryly.

As I began to scoot my chair next to his at the mixing desk to create the desired stereophonic pair of ears, I heard what he had said again in my mind—this time in an exaggerated "Beatles" voice. Oh, I get it. A joke as dry as a day-old scone.

Ahhhh . . . the British.

Abbey Road!

CLOSE MY EYES

I FEEL LIKE I'VE TALKED A LOT, HERE AND ELSEWHERE, about how much stock I put in the idea that almost all songs function in a way that consoles the listener with a brief but vital companionship. In essence taking the place of another human in the room—another consciousness filling the void of isolation. It's a tender relationship regardless of a song's musical nature. From the bleakest black metal to the sweetest pop confection. The power to embrace the lonely is always at the heart of the bargain.

I still believe that to be a rock-solid truth, but I also think that there's an equally important piece of humanity that some songs are uniquely efficient at teaching us about: empathy. It's kind of the same idea turned on its head, really. Instead of the listener's loneliness being acknowledged and erased, some songs remind us that there are other people out there NOT like us, going through things we can't fathom.

They need us, too—they deserve to be seen and we should work to understand them. The amazing thing is, some songs can perform this beautiful task without our even knowing or buying into the effort consciously. Here's how I think that works—we sing along in our heads, and when a song is in the first person, our minds hear us say "I" a lot. Now, I'm not sure if you are aware of this, but the "I" word carries a ton of fucking weight in our psyches. I picture anthropomorphized brain cells scrambling—"Is he singing about us! When did this happen?!? Let's get some images together ASAP. Feelings?! You MF-ers up?!? There we go. Crying now."

So it just sort of happens, I think. We know it's not us. But some part of who we are identifies it as "us," because we just experienced it the only way we know how—with access to only one consciousness. Because we have no choice. We're all kind of locked inside of ourselves with only one channel to watch. Everything is us. But some songs have the ability to sneak someone else's point of view past the well-guarded gates of our egos. And I think that how little our own intent matters makes it more powerful—we don't have to say to ourselves, "I'm going to work on identifying with a closeted gay teenager from Iowa today." But a song like "Close My Eyes" by Arthur Russell not only puts us in someone else's shoes, it bends down and ties them for us.

Arthur Russell wrote this song sometime in the eighties but it wasn't released until 2008, long after his death in 1992. It's a simple country-folk song just about at the opposite end of the spectrum from the experimental cello-driven dance music Russell was more well-known for.

Initially, I was sucker-punched by the song's warmth and charm compared to the icier music I was expecting. But it wasn't long before the words began seeping in—setting up shop. Putting me many steps closer to understanding what it feels like to be a closeted gay teenager growing up in rural Iowa. Closer to seeing through his eyes. And my having been taught to see this way made the song more human. Which has a funny way of making the "other" more human to me forever. Both of us now safer from my former ignorance and misunderstanding.

I close my eyes and listen
To hear the corn come out
Don't you hear the stars they glisten
As we go in and out
Down where the trees grow together
And the western path comes to an end
See the sign it says clear weather
I'll meet you tonight, my friend
Will the corn be growing a little tonight
As I wait in the fields for you
Who knows what grows in the morning light
When we can feel the watery dew

I just can't be there with no other
I know those hills will be true
Away from my sister and brother
Down through the grasses so new
The air is sweet and steady
And flowers bloom out of sight
I know the sky is ready
Come meet me down here tonight
Will the corn be growing a little tonight
As I wait in the fields for you
Who knows what grows in the morning light
As we can feel the watery dew

HAPPY BIRTHDAY

I SHOULD LOVE THIS SONG.

Reason 1: It's the ultimate folk song in that it's almost never sung in a formal setting. No one goes to a recital to see a guy in a tux sing "Happy Birthday." "Until you've heard Pavarotti sing it, you'll never truly appreciate it. By the time he got to the 'You belong in a zoo' part I had tears streaming down my cheeks." Outside of the waitstaff at TGI Fridays, no one gets paid to sing "Happy Birthday."

Reason 2: Obviously there are no other contenders for a song more often sung to us on joyous occasions. Ditto for songs sung to loved ones on their special day.

The sad truth is, I'm pretty ambivalent about this song. I'd even go so far as to say that I actively disdain singing it more often than not. I think things started to shift for me about the same time I started making records and being a musician began to be more legitimate in the eyes of my extended family members. Which is when I began to notice people looking at me as we gathered around the candle glow of a birthday cake and expecting me to "wow" them with my vocal chops. "Why isn't he leading us?" and "I can barely hear him, this is how he makes a living?" and "Doesn't seem like he knows the words" are just a few of the things I've suspected people were thinking.

I'm not alone, though. I have a nephew who struggles with the sensory overload of his relatives breaking out into song and ruining a perfectly enticing cake experience. He had grown to hate the song so much that on other family birthdays, we give his mom and dad enough of a heads-up to allow them to escort him out of earshot. One year on Susie's birthday, even being taken to the farthest corner of our backyard wasn't enough to prevent the mirthful strains of "Happy Birthday" from reaching his ears and causing a fairly major meltdown.

After some backroom counseling, he regained his composure enough to rejoin us at the table. At which point he calmly announced that he had something very important to share as he bit into his first bite of cake: "I hate all of you." Amen. Sometimes it takes someone brave enough to tell us the truth.

BANANA PANCAKE RECIPE

LATE NINETIES. BEING ASKED TO GO TO JOHN CALE'S home to write with him. Knocking on his door. Expecting him to be in black and white like the back cover of a Velvet Underground album. Being jarred by the man in shorts and a neon-pink tank top answering the door. John Cale in color. His idea—let's put a recipe to music.

Me, smart person, suggesting the banana pancake recipe located near the front of *Gravity's Rainbow*. Which I was familiar with because it fell within the zone of pages I had read before eventually giving up on the rest of the book, something that happened at least seven or eight times. Playing acoustic guitar while John Cale read aloud with his Welsh accent, which was totally familiar to me from his records, "melt in the skillet. Peel more bananas, slice lengthwise . . ."

Still feeling like this is more made up or dreamed than real. No evidence it ever happened . . . but it did.

LOVE LIKE A WIRE

HAVE YOU EVER HEARD A CONSTANT BUZZING BACK-ground radiation of regret whispering in your ear, saying, "You blew it"? Boy, I sure have.

In this case, I have a very particular type of ruing hanging around taunting me—the kind where you thought you had all the time in the world to tell someone what they mean to you, and then you blink, and they're gone. Gone-forever gone. Like dead gone.

It's a painful lesson. And I guess it's a pretty hard one to avoid. But that doesn't stop me from feeling awful about never telling Diane Izzo how great she was. I had chances—not a lot of them, but more than one would need to just say "Dang, you write great songs." If I had been listening closer, giving her the amount of undivided attention she deserved, I might have been able to hear her sing this song in person.

But I didn't. I took her for granted. We swam in the

same circles—played shows together, even. So, I had op-
portunities, before she died, to see her as she was: a
gifted songwriter and great human. She also happened
to write one of my favorite songs of all time, "Love Like
a Wire." Which makes this part even more difficult to
hear—believe it or not, the song was never officially recorded and released. So now I also regret writing about
a song you can't go and listen to. If you search for it online, you'll probably find some clips of me singing it. But
that's it.

I only know of this song because after she died, her
husband was working tirelessly to put together a tribute
record of other artists doing her songs. Through various
folks we have in common, I was handed a rough demo
of Diane's version as a guide for the version I was asked
to contribute. Hearing her sing these lyrics for the first
time—through layers of static and across years of warped
space and time—she sounded so alive. Maybe even
more alive than me in the moment. Because you have to
be really alive to sing something like this . . .

Climb out onto my burning rope
If they ask, you can say it was true love
If they ask, you can say you're the only one who bows
*   to love*

Sadly, her husband also passed away before he was
able to finish his project, and none of the tracks he was

lovingly assembling for the album in her memory have been released. I have some close friends working on ways to remedy that situation.

In the meantime, I've been working on not holding back in the moment. Ask any band that's toured with us in the last ten years or so. I think I freak a lot of them out when they get offstage, showering them with praise and encouragement. I mean it, too. It's such an honor to be a witness to someone else's art. Letting them know that all of the heart and soul they've put into their work is bright and visible is the least I can do.

I love getting to know other musicians, and it's weird to admit, but a lot of them care about my caring about them. I know they hear me and what I say is meaningful. Diane Izzo taught me to give it all up—every ounce of love. Before it's too late.

46

I LOVE YOU

AS THE SONGS I'M EXCITED TO WRITE ABOUT GET closer and closer to the present moment, I'm finding them more difficult to write about. Not because I think there's anything lacking. In my opinion there are always quality songs being written. And imparting my judgment, quality-wise, isn't even the main point of these chapters. This book is about how much we all can bring to a song as listeners—how we can make a bad song profound, dance to a song about death, hate a song because it "belongs" to a version of ourselves we'd rather not dwell upon or, worse yet, was a favorite of someone we'd rather not think about.

All of these things take time. The way it takes time to break in a new pair of jeans or new pair of shoes. Which is the best explanation I can come up with for why newly released music gets harder to talk about using the premise of this book. It's also a good explanation for why a lot of people start to believe that music just isn't as good as it was when they were younger. Like it's a real mystery why something you might overhear coming out of some kid's phone on a beach just doesn't stack up against the songs you listened to a thousand times a day, on headphones, at THE specific moment in your life your hormones started doing their thing—you know, the music you've already formed a bond with. Why isn't other music as good as that? Right?!

I've got bad (good?) news if you're thinking that kind of nonsense—it's you. Sorry, it is. It's not that there's no good music being made. It's you. You might be getting old. Because I'm here to tell you music is generally good stuff. A song that works usually keeps working. New songs find new people. And they tend to find the people who need them the most. Sometimes I hear new artists and think, "Oh, I wish I could hear what's really going on here." But it's not really for me. I'm not saying I'm being intentionally excluded or that it would necessarily be wrong if I were. Cool trick if you can create something that enforces its own boundaries as it makes its way into the world.

Punk rock set out to police its own borders, but to no avail. People found it, saw themselves in it, and before long you had a CBGB's gift shop at LaGuardia. Along the way it passed through the hands of all sorts of creeps. Neo-Nazis, in particular, found it irresistible. Probably because of the implied intention to segregate and piss off the "right" people. None of that is worth exploring much further than it's already been explored. Agendas are pretty antithetical to music, in my opinion.

Okay, where was I? Correct. I was about to pat myself on the back for not being like that. Not being someone who thinks music is bad because my needs weren't taken into consideration. I'm serious, though. I worked through some stuff to figure that out, and I'm proud of it. And I'm rewarded for my effort to keep an open mind by all of the incredible stuff I get to hear because I went TO it instead of expecting it to come looking for me, hat in hand—"Excuse us, Mr. Tweedy, would you find us more interesting and authentic if we incorporated some electric guitar?"

Not being ridiculous about one's own expectations gives us older folks a chance to appreciate someone like Billie Eilish and her brother, Finneas, for what they truly are: impeccably gifted stylists whose unique talents would have propelled them to stardom in almost any era of modern music. They make hyperreal pop music using digital technology and mic-ing techniques that emphasize the twists and turns of a quiet vocal to the point where a single cracked syllable becomes an arena-sized gesture. (It's possible they invented ASMR pop, although I think my friend Feist might have a stronger claim.)

And yet for all of their modernity, it's easy to picture almost any of their songs being sung leaning on a piano in some tiny jazz club. Which I guess is a way of saying that I did, in fact, find something specific in their music to relate to through the lens of my individual taste. True. But the point is, if you look for music that moves you, you're going to end up finding a way into more music than you might think.

One of the things I've gotten into the habit of doing when I hear a song I love is to pick up my guitar and see if I can learn it. To me it's a way to get one step closer to a song and a songwriter, and I feel privileged to have the ability to access other people's songs by playing them.

What I heard when I played this song to myself was nowhere near as pleasing to my ears as Billie's version. I'm a happy husband and father of two—I'm far away from the world she's living in, and the heartsick circumstances her lyrics are so directly addressing, so it struck me as odd that I could feel them so deeply as my own.

But music is the only language really being spoken here. And when a melody is this profound and beautiful, it makes belief transferable. She and her brother believed it enough for all of us to feel it. There is no greater feat a songwriter can achieve. When a song works this well, we're not only not alone anymore, we are in the presence of greatness.

PORTLAND STORY

HOW AFTER MANY YEARS OF VISITING CITIES AROUND the world, I've developed repetitive patterns and maybe even what would be considered rituals in many of them.

Returning to the exact spots I know I've been to in the past gives me a feeling of grounding that would otherwise get depleted by a nomadic lifestyle. I'm comforted by retracing my steps.

For example—many, many years ago, just before *Being There* came out, I was in Portland, Maine, where Bob Ludwig was mastering our record. One evening I went for a walk on a paved path that runs alongside the narrow-gauge railroad next to the briny water of Casco Bay. Just past a sewage treatment plant and right as the trail began to descend underneath a highway overpass, I came across a makeshift memorial. Some plastic flowers, burned-down candles, a couple of crosses, a teddy bear, and a few xeroxed photos of some kids who appeared to be teenagers. Rain had splotched and warped the smiling faces and names on the pages beyond easy recognition, but "Rest in Peace" remained remarkably clear. Everything else—the flowers, the candles, the teddy bear—all still radiated with a fresh vitality. This had just happened.

Back in my hotel room later that evening, I researched to the best of my ability and the midnineties internet's capability what might have happened to these kids. Morbid curiosity? Maybe. But I felt compelled nonetheless.

I learned that four were killed. I learned their names. Make of their automobile. Early morning. Single-car crash. Prom.

Nearly every visit to Portland since, I've made the trek out to visit the same spot.

The first time after my first encounter, the memorial had been formalized with a stone bench and a plaque with three names. Each followed by the familiar year-to-year span that indicates a lifetime. One life that lasted sixteen years. And two that had managed an extra year. In the weeds nearby, some of the original plastic flowers were still keeping watch.

Second revisit seemed to have coincided with some anniversary or possibly a birthday. Fresh flowers. New teddy bear.

That was the last time any of my visits have provided physical evidence of any loved ones tending to their memory. Although I'm sure someone somewhere is still thinking about them.

I mean, besides me.

One visit, maybe ten or twelve years ago, was the first time I had trouble locating "the spot." Roadside vegetation had engulfed the stone bench, and it took some kicking around in the weeds and brush to uncover it.

The last few times, nothing. Somehow the bench has disappeared. I've looked carefully at the rocks and debris nearby, hopeful I could find some smaller pieces of a former bench that had been broken down by weather or perhaps vandalized. It's gone.

But it's not. I still think about it. And them. I even remember the fourth name that had been left off the plaque.

So why share such a sad and brutal tale of mortality and how nearby oblivion looms?

Because I'm still here. And I can. And they can't tell you. They didn't get the chance.

I love them.

And I love seeing where I've been and being reminded I'm still here.

WHO LOVES THE SUN

IN THE EARLY 2000S, LOOSE FUR, A BAND JIM O'ROURKE, Glenn Kotche, and I had started mostly to document the music that seemed to spontaneously compose itself whenever the three of us were in the same room at the same time, played a couple of shows in New York. They ended up being the only real shows we ever played. And one of the nights was also the only time I'm aware of that I performed for Lou Reed.

Thankfully, I wasn't apprised of his presence until after the show. Knowing he was out there would have wrecked me like almost no one else could have. So I'm grateful to whoever made the call to keep it under wraps. It was a big deal to me. The biggest deal you can imagine. To put it in perspective, imagine someone coming up to you after a Little League baseball game and saying, "Hey, guess what? Babe Ruth was in the stands," or after a grade school performance of *Bye Bye Birdie*, maybe someone tells you, "Shakespeare was here! I saw him tapping his foot."

So Lou Reed was there, and for a brief moment at least, he was aware of my existence. Which is ridiculous to care about. But I do, so sue me. We never met and I'm pretty okay with that, considering how awful his reputation was when it came to making people feel like shit. I have met his wife, Laurie Anderson, a few times, and she is the absolute best. So warm and inviting. And that makes me think Lou couldn't have been all that bad.

Still, just knowing he was at a show I played feels complete to me, and it also sidesteps the likelihood he might have called me a schmuck or made me cry with a withering stare. It's hard to explain how one grumpy dude could wield so much perceived power—make so many people unsure of their own worth and fear his judgment. I think it has something to do with this: To a lot of us, Lou Reed represents the triumph of form over beauty, ideas over sentiment, honesty over bullshit, vision over acceptance. He flipped off all of the phonies for us. And he made it clear who the phonies were, and underlined how little technical perfection mattered if all you were going to do with it was pander to the powers that be.

He possessed the rawest form of raw talent—the ability to shape the world around him to meet his own ends. It's a terrifying power. Of course, when you dig through history there are lots of Lou Reeds. They're the ones who remind people that the world doesn't have to be this way. And even more important, they're the ones who remind every misfit alive that fitting in isn't all it's cracked up to be, so you might as well step out into the light.

Which brings us back to why it's such a daunting prospect to be deemed "less than" and humiliated by the guy who gave you permission to be yourself in the first place. How agonizing would it be to have Lou Reed say, in effect, "No, not you! Everyone else. Junkies, deviants, misanthropes, Metallica . . . Yes! You? No. You suck!"

So, "Who Loves the Sun"? Apparently "not everyone," as the song says. Which, taken purely at face value, feels like a high five to this beach skeptic. Of course, it means much more than that. Like a sizable majority of the VU catalog, this song asks the question, "Am I not fitting in?" and before anyone can answer, we get the rhetorical follow-up, "So what!?"

You see the word "misanthrope" get used a lot in relation to the overall impression Lou Reed made on the world. But I think there was an incredible positivity to the Velvet Underground that goes against all the sordid narratives of decadence and societal decay. I mean, that's pretty obvious by now, right? What entered in as deviance and subversiveness ended up being paid out in acceptance and consolation for a fuck-ton of people. Before the internet, this was how people found each other and formed families without blood ties.

That, in my opinion, was the great revolutionary leap this band made. It was the opening of the doors of inclusion to so many weirdos like me. You know, alienated but not all that weird really. And even bigger, more legit weirdos. It wasn't the championing of drugs or sexual transgression. Not the darkness. It didn't speak solely to the participants of subterranean pursuits. No. I look at it more in a sheep-in-wolf's-clothing kind of way—"Yes, we are wearing dark clothes. We are very scary. Let's look at the seamy underbelly of life together, shall we?" but the "TOGETHER" part ended up being the subtle affirming subtext most people heard—"Oh, you'd like that? Well, make yourself right at home."

What their records did was offer a legitimate and believable ray of sunlight to those who would never stomach being pandered to with talk of togetherness and love. For people burdened by their own minds who stumbled upon these records (at any point, from the day they were released to yesterday), life got a tiny bit easier. The Velvet Underground (and let's face it, Andy Warhol) plowed the fields with a clear strategy for living. Accept your friends. Make some art with your friends. Support them even when they sort of suck sometimes. There. You have a family. Now go forth and proliferate.

I'M INTO SOMETHING GOOD

HAS THERE EVER BEEN A MORE EFFERVESCENT SONG than this Carole King–penned Herman's Hermits hit? I don't think so. It's like the opposite of the blues. What would that be color-wise? Yellow? As in: "Hey, man, what are you smiling about?"—"Who, me? Dunno, I guess I've just got the yellows."

Point is, it's delightful and I love it. And what makes me love it even more is the fact that it's my wife Susie's favorite song from her childhood. Or at least it was until I ruined it for her. Back before we were married, when I first learned of her deep affection for all things Peter Noone (Herman) and "I'm into Something Good" specifically, I set out to impress her by learning it on guitar so I could sing it for her and make her swoon.

Problem is, I learned it wrong. It went like this: One day we're sitting around just hanging out and I go, "Hey, Susie, check it out!" and I start singing, "Woke up this morning feeling fine . . ." Instantly, Susie is up off the couch singing along and doing some sort of era-specific *Hullabaloo* dance. I'm thinking to myself, "I now know the secret to unearthing unlimited joy at any moment." I felt like how one of those snake charmers must feel the first time they get a cobra to stand up in a basket and do a jig with their flute. Don't tell Susie I compared her to a cobra.

Okay. Things were going great. Then I realized I only really learned the first part of the song. So I stretched out the last "Something tells me I'm into something goooooooood" before I got to the cliff's edge of unknown chords and lyrics and stopped. How did Susie respond, you ask? "Crestfallen" is a word that comes to mind. But that doesn't really convey the implicit anger I was sensing. Susie stopped dancing and moaned, "What gives?!?" like the preteen girl she had just morphed into.

Now, instead of cutting my losses and telling her I'd learn the rest later, I decided to press on. "How hard could it be?" I thought, knowing vaguely where the song was headed from memory. As I stumbled through wrong chords and wrong lyrics, Susie looked on, shaking her head like a rabbi aghast at a bar mitzvah's mangling of their haftarah. Which isn't far off for her, really. What I was doing was sacrilegious. I was desecrating a sacred text.

So here's where things get weird. I have seriously tried, repeatedly, to learn this song correctly, to redeem myself in the eyes of the love of my life, but it eludes me. There's something about how it all goes together that doesn't make sense to me. Or maybe I've just been conditioned to self-sabotage whenever I get close to the scene of the crime—let's call it "the bridge."

Luckily, my failure to nail this one song down has become a running family joke. The joke being that I start singing the song, Susie gets excited, I fuck it up, and Susie gets comically furious.

At least I think it's a joke. In a way it's fitting. That song belongs to her and whatever imaginary (don't tell her I called it imaginary) relationship she has with Herman or Peter Noone (or Peter No One, as I like to call him). I could never compete with the purity of a pop music fantasy. And why bother, when we have the real thing?

HEART OF GLASS

FINDING OUT MY BROTHER WAS HAVING SERIOUS HEART problems from my sister on the phone backstage at an outdoor venue in Montana.

As I'm hanging up, I see a car slow down and stop on a service road parallel to the security fencing. A man gets out and starts running toward me, shouting my name.

Against my normal instinct to hide, I wait for him at the fence. He says he wants to give me something.

Still shaken up from the news of my brother's grim situation, I wait as he runs back to his car to retrieve the item he wants me to have.

Before he unveils my gift, I'm told a bit about his personal history and how my music fits into his own salvation. Short story: Did a lot of drugs. Ended up in jail. Got clean (with the help of *Sky Blue Sky*, he says). Learned the art of glassblowing in prison and now teaches glassblowing to prisoners. As he talks, I begin to really feel connected to the guy. Can't explain it other than maybe family was already on my mind. Whatever it is, this man and his story start feeling like they belong to some shared family history. My mother collected glass paperweights when she was alive, and his mention of glassblowing surely led my mind to her memory.

I start picturing the color red as he talks on. My mother's favorite color. I picture the countless ruby-red glass eggs, globes, and obelisks that occupied entire shelves of her collection. Before he stops talking I know what he's going to give me. I can see it clearly in my mind's eye.

I'm not particularly prone to this type of thing. I believe in a lot, but when things get outright magical, I resist. But here's the thing—I love that we can have these moments that might be better explained by the reality that coincidences occur and the world would be much weirder if nothing ever lined up in lovely serendipitous circles and parallels—moments that nonetheless feel profound, meaningful, and outside of normal explanation. I think it's important we remain open to these moments. Recognizing that we sometimes need things to NOT just make sense. We're desperately in need of experiences that blow our minds with wonder and humble us back into our place in the scary beautiful cosmic mystery we're all blindly swimming around in.

He hands me the gift he brought with him to the show in the hopes that we'd meet.

Slowly unwrapping a heart-sized, crimson, hand-blown glass paperweight.

My dead mother's heart. My sick brother's heart. My sister's heart. My heart.

I wept.

It's on my amp every night.

I'M BEGINNING
TO SEE THE LIGHT

I never cared much for moonlit skies
I never winked back at fireflies
But now that the stars are in your eyes
I'm beginning to see the light

I learned this Duke Ellington, Johnny Hodges, Harry James, and Don George–penned song from a cheap compilation CD of early Ellington tracks.

There's a more famous version, sung by Ella Fitzgerald, but Joya Sherrill is the vocalist on this version, the one that stole my heart. The starry-eyed feeling of falling in love in spite of one's defenses—the melting away of a jaded exterior—so clearly stated with simple visual metaphors and similes. It's madly romantic. Too-good-to-be-true lyricism that makes even the faintest smile audible. No matter who's singing.

Which is just one of the reasons I started singing it to

Spencer and Sammy at bedtime. A great song works even when repurposed for familial love. And I've never found a song that better expressed the feeling of wonder I had at discovering the deep abiding love I have for my children. Nothing prepared me for that. And this song helped me make sense of it a little bit. Sure, it's a song to be sung lover to lover. But that never bothered me. Even when the lyrics hit the romance side a little too square on the head, it really doesn't matter when you're singing to a couple of little humans who can light even the darkest days.

I'LL TAKE YOU THERE

HERE'S SOMETHING THAT ANYONE WHO'S EVER BEEN
over to our house knows. At some point in the evening,
Susie is going to turn on the incredible 1957 Seeburg
jukebox I bought her for her fiftieth birthday and punch
B-12, the ceremonial first number of any dance party in
the Tweedy household. "I'll Take You There" by the
Staple Singers. This began even before we had any relationship with the woman herself.

The actual 45 being loaded onto the spindle belonged
to Susie as a kid, way before jukebox life. It's amazing
how Mavis Staples and her family were woven into our
lives so deeply that when I finally met her, it felt like a
reunion. Even stranger, she felt it, too. It just felt like we
were family right off the bat. Which I think says a lot
more about Mavis and the way she's been able to openly
embrace the world around her than it does about us.
We're just a couple of people among the millions who

have fallen in love with her, and with each other with Mavis by our side. I've gotten close enough to her over the years to watch her welcome other strangers like long-lost kin, so I know there's a little bit of wish casting going on. But we did hit it off enough to make a lot of music together.

One of the first discussions Mavis and I ever had on the phone, when we were still feeling for a way to collaborate, led us to the notion that as far apart as we may seem to the outside world in terms of genre and life experience, what we had in common was far more important—the idea that all anyone is really accomplishing by lifting up their voice in song is to let the world know they're here. Not to show off or brag or put one over on anyone. But because it made us feel better.

And we both understood that any song worth singing could never have begun with our singular voices. We both believed in something much larger than a single voice or song, something we knew from experience. When we had been alone, the songs sung to us unlocked us from our isolation. And allowed us to sing. Our own songs? Maybe. But nothing so important could be or should be believed to be wholly owned by anyone.

Mavis and I wrote a song together to reflect our shared sweet, hopeful understanding of what it actually is that we do when we sing and when others listen to our songs. It has to do with loneliness, and how much of it there is. I'm here. You're here. That's all that can really be said.

It's heartbreaking and simple. Uplifting and difficult. So, we wrote our first song together to acknowledge the core task at hand. "You Are Not Alone." I personally think of this song in an extremely literal sense. I imagine it's because I spent so much time factually alone in my bedroom being comforted by my record collection. So I always picture any type of person you can imagine—headbanger, goth kid, accountant—alone in a room, confronting a faded connection with the world, being told by our song exactly what I most wanted every song to tell me. You. Are. Not. Alone.

It's a wonderful feeling to have a hand on your shoulder. What else is there?

Every time Susie and I dance in our living room to "I'll Take You There," I'm reminded of how sweet it was of Mavis to not remind me that she'd been singing our song way before we wrote it. But then again, she gets it. She knows that it's not something you do once and then you're done. You don't get "there" and stay. Every day, you get up and search for it again. Mavis knows the way. We all do. You just have to sing along.

ACKNOWLEDGMENTS

Even though I believe that I've stated clearly enough throughout this book that my primary objective has not been to provide an overview of songs and songwriters I judge to be of the greatest value to all, I'm still feeling a bit queasy when I think of some of this book's most egregious omissions: Your Neil Youngs . . . your Lana Del Reys . . . your Smokey Robinsons . . . your Kurt Cobains . . . your Arethas . . . your Cohens, and your Yankovics . . . I honestly could go on for at least another one thousand pages.

So with one last plea for forgiveness to the acknowledgment gods and goddesses for all of the unintentionally overlooked beauty and inspiration, I'd like to first bow deeply to all of the artists past, present, and future, who shape not just me but my own songs, and then by extension, anyone kind enough to listen closely when I sing. It's truly a wonder to be a part of something so vast and imposing yet able to fit through the smallest cracks in any human heart. It's the only club I've ever really wanted to belong to. I know there aren't dues or oaths to take or any prerequisites . . . and no one asked me to join. Nonetheless, it is a massive collection of humanity I cherish counting myself among, that dream-bent and magically flawed sub-phylum of musicians known as songwriters. In "Tower of Song," Leonard Cohen claims Hank Williams lives a hundred floors above him. Whenever I hear that lyric, I think about how happy I am to have found a place for myself in that same "Tower" by way of a small sublet room in the unfinished basement.

All I'm saying is—I owe a lot to a lot of people who aren't mentioned. I wish I could tell you all everything about what they all mean to me. But I can't. Plus, that wouldn't leave me enough space to acknowledge you. Which is hopefully the clearest message made by these pages. What we individually bring to a song matters a lot. In the economy of listening, a song is worth whatever WE make of it. So while this book is technically about the songs I'm made of, and what I've made of the songs I've loved (and hated), none of it would make any sense without the faith I have in everyone's ability to absorb and be absorbed by music.

Including yours. So thank you. Good job!

SONG CREDITS

"Smoke on the Water"
Written by Ritchie Blackmore, Ian Gillan, Roger Glover,
    Jon Lord, and Ian Paice
Recorded by Deep Purple
From the album *Machine Head* (Purple Records, 1972)

"Long Tall Glasses"
Written by Leo Sayer and David Courtney
Recorded by Leo Sayer
From the album *Just a Boy* (Chrysalis, 1974)

"Takin' Care of Business"
Written by Randy Bachman
Recorded by Bachman-Turner Overdrive
From the album *Bachman-Turner Overdrive II*
    (Mercury, 1973)

"Don't Think Twice, It's All Right"
Written and recorded by Bob Dylan
From the album *The Freewheelin' Bob Dylan*
    (Columbia, 1963)

"Mull of Kintyre"
Written by Paul McCartney and Denny Laine
Recorded by Wings
From the album *Wings Greatest* (Capitol, 1978)

"Loud, Loud, Loud"
Written by Vangelis Papathanassiou and Costas Ferris
Recorded by Aphrodite's Child
From the album *666* (Vertigo, 1972)

"Both Sides Now"
Written and recorded by Joni Mitchell
From the album *Clouds* (Reprise, 1969)

"Lucky Number"
Written by Lene Lovich and Les Chappell
Recorded by Lene Lovich
From the album *Stateless* (Stiff, 1978)

"Gloria"
Written by Patti Smith and Van Morrison
Recorded by Patti Smith
From the album *Horses* (Arista, 1975)

"As If It Always Happens"
Written and recorded by Slovenly
From the album *Riposte* (SST, 1987)

"Somewhere Over the Rainbow"
Written by E. Y. Harburg and Harold Arlen
Recorded by Judy Garland
From the album *The Wizard of Oz* (Decca, 1940)

"Death or Glory"
Written by Joe Strummer and Mick Jones
Recorded by The Clash
From the album *London Calling* (CBS, 1979)

"My Sharona"
Written by Doug Fieger and Berton Averre
Recorded by The Knack
From the album *Get the Knack* (Capitol, 1979)

"In Germany Before the War"
Written by Randy Newman
Recorded by Randy Newman
From the album *Little Criminals* (Warner Bros., 1977)

"Dancing Queen"
Written by Benny Andersson, Björn Ulvaeus,
    and Stig Anderson
Recorded by ABBA
From the album *Arrival* (Atlantic, 1976)

"The Message"
Written by Edward G. Fletcher, Melle Mel, Clifton
    "Jiggs" Chase, and Sylvia Robinson
Recorded by Grandmaster Flash and the Furious Five
From the album *The Message* (Sugar Hill, 1982)

"Balancing Act"
Written by Peter Prescott
Recorded by Volcano Suns
From the album *The Bright Orange Years*
    (Homestead Records, 1985)

"Frankie Teardrop"
Written by Alan Vega and Martin Rev
Recorded by Suicide
From the album *Suicide* (Red Star, 1977)

"I'm Not in Love"
Written by Graham Gouldman and Eric Stewart
Recorded by 10cc
From the album *The Original Soundtrack* (Mercury, 1975)

"Connection"
Written by Mick Jagger and Keith Richards
Recorded by The Rolling Stones
From the album *Between the Buttons*
    (Decca/ABKCO UK, London/ABKCO US, 1967)

"Forever Paradise"
Written by J. J. O'Neill
Recorded by The Undertones
From the album *Positive Touch* (Harvest, 1981)

"Satan, Your Kingdom Must Come Down"
Recorded by Frank Proffitt
From the album *High Atmosphere: Ballads and*
    Banjo Tunes from Virginia and North Carolina
    (Rounder Records, 1975)

"God Damn Job"
Written by Paul Westerberg
Recorded by The Replacements
From the EP *Stink* (Twin/Tone, 1982)

"Ramblin' Man"
Written by Dickey Betts
Recorded by The Allman Brothers Band
From the album *Brothers and Sisters* (Capricorn, 1973)

"History Lesson—Part II"
Written by Mike Watt
Recorded by Minutemen
From the album *Double Nickels on the Dime* (SST, 1984)

"Little Johnny Jewel"
Written by Tom Verlaine
Recorded by Television
From the album *Marquee Moon* (Bonus Tracks)
    (Elektra, 2003)

"4'33""
Composed by John Cage

"Anchorage"
Written by Michelle Shocked
Recorded by Michelle Shocked
From the album *Short Sharp Shocked* (Mercury, 1988)

"(Sittin' on) The Dock of the Bay"
Written by Steve Cropper and Otis Redding
Recorded by Otis Redding
From the single "(Sittin' on) The Dock of the Bay"
    (Stax Records, 1968)

"You Are My Sunshine"
Performed by The Carter Family
From the album *The Carter Family on Border Radio*,
    vol. 3: 1939 (Arhoolie Records, 1999)

"I Will Always Love You"
Written by Dolly Parton
Recorded by Dolly Parton
From the album *Jolene* (RCA Victor, 1974)

"Wanted Dead or Alive"
Written by Jon Bon Jovi and Richie Sambora
Recorded by Jon Bon Jovi
From the album *Slippery When Wet* (Mercury, 1987)

"Before Tonight"
Written by Joe Adducci
From the album *Notes Campfire* (Moll Tonträger, 1996)

"Shotgun"
Written by Autry DeWalt (Junior Walker)
Recorded by Junior Walker & the All Stars
From the single "Shotgun" (Soul Records, 1965)

"The Weight"
Written by Robbie Robertson
Recorded by The Band
From the album *Music from Big Pink* (Capitol, 1968)

"Will You Love Me Tomorrow"
Written by Gerry Goffin and Carole King
Recorded by The Shirelles
From the album *Tonight's the Night* (Scepter, 1960)

"Free Bird"
Written by Allen Collins and Ronnie Van Zant
Recorded by Lynyrd Skynyrd
From the album *(Pronounced 'Lĕh-'nérd 'Skin-'nérd)*
    (MCA, 1973)

"The Star-Spangled Banner"
Written by Francis Scott Key
    (from his poem "Defence of Fort M'Henry")
Set to the tune of "To Anacreon in Heaven"
    by John Stafford Smith

"Radio Free Europe"
Written by Bill Berry, Peter Buck, Mike Mills,
    and Michael Stipe
Recorded by R.E.M.
From the album *Murmur* (I.R.S., 1983)

"I'm Against It"
Written by Douglas Colvin, John Cummings,
    and Jeff Hyman
Recorded by Ramones
From the album *Road to Ruin* (Sire, 1978)

"Bizcochito"
Written by Rosalía Vila, David Rodríguez,
   and Michael Uzowuru
Recorded by Rosalía
From the album *Motomami* (Columbia, 2022)

"Close My Eyes"
Written by Arthur Russell
Recorded by Arthur Russell
From the album *Love Is Overtaking Me* (Audika, 2008)

"Happy Birthday"

"Love Like a Wire"
Written by Diane Izzo

"I Love You"
Written by Billie Eilish O'Connell and Finneas O'Connell
Recorded by Billie Eilish
From the album *When We All Fall Asleep, Where Do We Go?*
   (Darkroom, 2019)

"Who Loves the Sun"
Written by Lou Reed
Recorded by The Velvet Underground
From the album *Loaded* (Cotillion, 1970)

"I'm into Something Good"
Written by Gerry Goffin and Carole King
Recorded by Herman's Hermits
From the album *Herman's Hermits* (MGM, 1964)

"I'm Beginning to See the Light"
Written by Duke Ellington, Don George, Johnny Hodges,
    and Harry James
Recorded by Duke Ellington and his orchestra, with vocals
    by Joya Sherrill
From the single "I'm Beginning to See the Light"
    (RCA, 1944)

"I'll Take You There"
Written by Al Bell
Recorded by The Staple Singers
From the album *Be Altitude: Respect Yourself* (Stax, 1972)

PERMISSIONS

Excerpts of lyrics from the following songs have been reproduced herein by arrangement with the music publishers:

"Don't Think Twice, It's All Right"
Written by Bob Dylan
© 1963 Universal Tunes
Reprinted by permission of Hal Leonard LLC

"Loud, Loud, Loud"
Written by Constantinos Costas Ferris and
    Evanghelos Papathanassiou
© 1972 Intersong USA, Inc.

"Gloria: In Excelsis Deo"
Written by Patti Smith
© 1975 Linda's Music

ABOUT THE AUTHOR

As the founding member and leader of the Grammy Award–winning American rock band Wilco, and before that the cofounder of the alt-country band Uncle Tupelo, **Jeff Tweedy** is one of contemporary music's most accomplished songwriters, musicians, and performers. Jeff has released two solo albums, has written original songs for twelve Wilco albums, and is the author of the *New York Times* bestsellers *Let's Go (So We Can Get Back): A Memoir of Recording and Discording with Wilco, Etc.* and *How to Write One Song*. He lives in Chicago with his family.